# Trick and
# Fancy Riding

Frank and Bernice Dean. Frank completing a Crupper to a Stand, Bernice doing a Backward Hippodrome Stand

# Trick
## and
# Fancy Riding

## by
## Frank E. Dean

The CAXTON PRINTERS, Ltd.
Caldwell, Idaho   83605
1975

First printing, 1960
Second printing, February, 1975

LIBRARY OF CONGRESS CATALOG NUMBER: 60-13312

INTERNATIONAL STANDARD BOOK NUMBER 0-87004-240-8

Lithographed and bound in the United States of America by
The CAXTON PRINTERS, Ltd.
Caldwell, Idaho 83605
121638

## DEDICATION

This book is dedicated not only to all trick riders, past, present and future, but to my wife Bernice who has patiently worked with me to complete it.

# CONTENTS

**PHOTO CREDITS:**

Frontis, O'Neill; p. 35, p. 97, p. 119, p. 133, p. 158, p. 166, p. 222, p. 224, p. 225, Ernie Mack; p. 41, p. 73, p. 122, George Baker; p. 56, p. 232, DeVere; p. 70, p. 78, p. 183, p. 222, Doubleday; p. 81, J. B. Harris; p. 93, Bone; p. 164, p. 185, Pavley; p. 223, Stryker. Rest by author or unidentified.

## PREFACE

THERE HAS BEEN NO PREVIOUS ATTEMPT to cover the entire scope of riding stunts accomplished by the Rodeo contest trick rider.

To successfully record these feats of skill has taken the greater part of a lifetime. Some one had to do it. Unbelievable stunts performed at Rodeo Contests in the past could have been lost forever. That they are not lost is due in part to the many co-operative people who have furnished the author much of the background material used in this text.

Ben Pitti, who was active in stunt work from 1910 on the Young Buffalo Wild West Show to his death in 1957, Ken Maynard, famous Motion Picture Star and former champion trick rider, "Smokey" Chism, George Pittman, Louie and Bernadette Cabral, Ed and Tillie Bowman, Dick Griffith, Betsy Ross and J. King Ross, every one with a knowledge of trick riding and every one immeasurably helpful.

J. King Ross and his daughter, Betsy Ross Day, and Mary Peterson are due even greater consideration for these long-time friends have helped us overcome many obstacles.

Some of the rarest photos were from the late R. R. Doubleday files. Doubleday started taking Rodeo action photos before the turn of the century and covered about a forty year period. Our stick men figures were drawn by Nick Tanno and the late cowboy artist Pete Dixon drew many of the line drawings.

As you read through the following chapters you will find many more names of grand people, all of whom, I feel, have done their part too.

# PART ONE:
# THE PRELIMINARIES

## 1. RIDING FUN FOR NOVICE OR EXPERT

TRICK RIDING IS FUN. It is exciting. It is a little strenuous, sometimes dangerous, and often without rhyme or reason. But, for a man and a horse who like to have fun together, there is nothing like it.

Not quite a sport or exactly a profession, not an after-dinner game, or an especially practical skill, it still captures the attention and imagination of horsemen and sportsmen everywhere. For trick riding, like other competitive sports, demonstrates a man's strength, his skill, his courage, and certainly his ability to ride anywhere and everywhere on a horse.

As long as there are horses and riders there will be trick riding. The day a boy tries to stand on his pony's back and finds it is easy he is on the road to trick riding. The day a beginner loses his stirrups and discovers he can ride without them he is ready to try some stunts. Trick riding grows by taking chances. All horsemen like to take chances. If they didn't they would stick to an easy chair instead of learning to ride in the first place.

And the nice part about trick riding is that anyone can do it. All you need is a horse and some nerve, plus the instructions in this book. With that equipment the field has unlimited possibilities. Try the simple or the difficult stunts, the choice is yours. You can develop your tricks as you wish, become elaborate, take a chance on suicide if you like, or merely concentrate on perfection of performance. Briefly, trick riding is acrobatics done on the back of a fast running saddle horse. Therefore you can pick up the tricks that suit your fancy, be they balancing, tumbling, vaulting, handstands, muscle stunts, or plain spinning around in mid-air.

Get off the saddle when your horse is running and you are trick riding. But, the more tricks you learn, the more gracefully you do them, and the faster your horse runs, the better trick rider you will be. There is no end to the possibilities. Knock yourself out, be a ballet dancer or a contortionist, but keep your horse running straight and fast.

1

Trick riding is American in that we have developed it to such a point through individual competition that the rest of the world tends to stand back and let us carry the title. Russian Cossacks run us a close second in the game, and of course the early Romans started it all.

The history of trick riding goes back to the first fellow who climbed on his horse in the conventional manner and decided it would be faster to make a running jump. A groom in the stables of Rome experimented with the idea of standing on a running horse and, by the fourth century, Romans were howling in the Circus Maximus at the horseraces in which the "jockeys" rode standing up. Later the armies of the world taught basic trick riding so that men would be better able to take care of themselves on horseback. The soldiers were taught to vault to their saddles, to pick up objects from the ground, perhaps a sword or a wounded comrade, and to do a "Hiddenride". This last named feat was a good deal similar to the present day Rodeo trick riders' "Fender Drag" and enabled the rider to provide a smaller, if not invisible, target for the enemy marksman.

It seemed logical then for a soldier to have been the first to make a profession of performing these daring stunts. An English Cavalryman, Sgt. Phillip Astley, formerly of the 15th Light Dragoons, put on a show near London in 1768—and to quote from the advertising of that time—"will exhibit several extraordinary feats on one, two, three, and four horses. These feats are in number upwards of fifty".

This number you will note was not done entirely on one horse but included combinations using up to four mounts.

The game caught on, but, to make it easier, large heavy horses were used and worked in a small circle under controlled speed and gait. From this was developed the "bareback" or "rosinback" type of riding which is well known in circuses today. Performers used nothing but a surcingle around the girth of the horse and powdered the back with rosin to make it sticky for standing. Real acrobatics such as flips and somersaults were done on the big horses.

And then came the American cowboy and the Cossacks. The cowboy had already experimented enough to be making flying and running mounts; most of them knew how to stand in the saddle, some knew how to vault. They liked it. In rodeos they held contests to see

2

who could do the most; but they were limited because of the small size of their western horses. When the Cossacks came to the United States for the World's Fair in Chicago in 1893, the Americans picked up some hints and bright ideas. From that date on trick riding had a boom from coast to coast.

The Russians knew how to tuck to a vault which gave them tremendous spring. They used saddles and straps to help them which the bareback riders had not used. Their horses were saddle horses and they were trained to run straight without swerving, regardless of what gymnastics the rider might be doing. Cowboys went home and gave their ponies a going over. They worked alone and did some inventing and some improving, took some spills, and came up with modern trick riding — which has been unequaled anywhere on earth.

Although the early riders had to experiment and take chances, the modern trick rider needs only to be told how the trick is done, take a deep breath, get his horse going, and do it. The improvement and development of new tricks is still a wide-open field, but the beginner will learn more tricks from this book than any living trick rider now can do. Every trick listed here has been done by someone, but no one person so far can do them all.

Some of these tricks are difficult, some will crack your skull if you do them wrong, many are easy, one or two will kill you if you get cocky — but are all interesting.

With the flat ground under you, a good level-headed horse that you trust, and a firm grip on some part of the saddle or horse, you are securely anchored and as free as a bird. Nothing on earth can compare with it. You don't need an audience to applaud you, or someone to pat you on the head and say "well done". When your feet hit the ground and you fly through the air, take a turn, and land solid in the saddle, you know what you have done and it makes you feel on top of the world.

Should you land in a heap in the dust, it is doubtful if you will be hurt, but you may be a little grimy. What of it? You have tackled something tough and that is a challenge. When you have licked the problem, done it right, and you and the horse come home together, you own the world — Ask any trick rider!

Although contest riding with its rewards in money, fame, and satisfaction is largely a thing of the past, it did much to promote enthusiasm for the sport. Contest riding was well started by 1910 and ran like wildfire until about 1935. During that period trick riders did everything to outride each other even to the point of occasionally getting their brains kicked out. As the judging of these contests gave 60% credit for speed of the horse, 30% for variety of of tricks, and only 10% for grace and neatness of the performance, riders went all out to do the almost impossible on horses that ran like deer. As they were penalized for an excessive number of hand holds, contest riders really took chances to win points.

Ted Elder became World's Champion Trick Rider at this time and managed to hold this title for many years by starting his horse running, assuming a standing position from which he did a back somersault to the ground to jump back to the saddle! He did this without a single special hand hold. His other title at this time was "Suicide".

When Dick Griffith captured the title he did a simple-sounding little stunt called a "Crupper Cartwheel". Unfortunately for the other contestants the stunt was far more difficult than its name. Nonchalantly he started his trick by merely jumping off the rump of the horse. Then as he sailed high he ducked his head down to the left of the horse, clamped his feet together in the air and went over forward. This time he hit the ground facing forward, swung through the air, lifted and twisted, and landed back astride the horse.

Not satisfied with the Crupper Cartwheel alone, he also did a neck-breaking stunt in which he jumped off the rump of the running horse, sailed high and straight in the air to land on his *head* on the saddle. He used no gadgets to help him.

In 1934 Tex Austin put on a rodeo in England featuring, among other things, a trick riding contest. Dick Griffith starred and this time he achieved the incredible total of 109 different tricks. They are all described in this text and they are not simple little things to be picked up on a Sunday afternoon. For both quality and quantity Griffith became International Trick Riding Champion.

4

Today trick riding is largely exhibition work as there are few if any contests now. Competition in a small way is still alive, since each rider resents being outdone whether there is a financial stake involved or not.

Nevertheless, the quarter of a century of contests was really responsible for the growth and development of the present number of trick-riding accomplishments. For instance, at the Columbian Exposition Rodeo in St. Louis in 1904, Jack Joyce won the trick-riding contest doing a total of only 4 tricks, but, here in this text nearly a half century later, we are going to describe more than 140 tricks and variations.

These are not all the tricks possible, but they represent more than most trick riders ever care to learn.

With the cunning and suspiciousness of a jewel collector, trick riders have always tried to keep secret their little bags of tricks. And with good reason. It is difficult to invent a really good trick — not only difficult but often painful. The method of placing the hands, the swing and the timing must all be worked out with the horse in motion. This means that any necessary changes in procedure for the successful performance are bluntly brought to the rider's attention as he lands sprawling on the face of the earth.

With that as the background for a new trick, the rider has every reason to try and keep the final and successful method a secret. During contest shows riders have been known to practice only at night when they could not be seen, and to keep their saddles with special hand holds hidden. Buck Stewart even went so far as to keep his horse covered with a cooler blanket, taking it off only at the last possible moment before he rode in front of the judges.

With the decline of trick riding contests in recent years, secrecy is no longer important and it is possible to reveal many of the methods used in trick riding without spoiling any of the hitherto jealously guarded secrets. Therefore this book (and especially its photographs) show exactly how tricks are done. We do not claim that these are the only ways to do them. Every rider has his own variations. But these are the basic and proven successful methods. You can carry on from there. Jackknife instead of tuck, hang by your teeth instead of by one foot, do what you please. No one can interfere with a trick rider. There are no restrictions, no bosses, no limits.

**Will Rogers, son Jimmie and daughter Mary, all doing the Hippodrome Stand**

## 2. SELECT A BROADMINDED HORSE

AS WAS SAID AT THE BEGINNING, all you need to trickride is a horse and a lot of nerve. It is, however, a help to have a good horse and very convenient to have a good saddle. As for the nerve, that comes naturally. Even the timid will gain confidence as they learn and the first fall will take the scare out of that. Falling is easy, merely a matter of gravity and bounce.

The horse can make the whole business a pleasure — even the falling part, should it occur. A good trick-riding horse is sympathetic and understanding. This type of mount may stop when he realizes his rider is hung up or perhaps jump over his fallen rider, if that becomes necessary.

A young, nervous animal, full of the fire of youth, may make a wonderful parade horse, but, as a trick-riding mount for a beginner, he'd make a good partner for an undertaker.

An experienced trick rider and horseman might do very well with such a horse. The tyro trick rider, however, would waste lots of time with the young, flighty, or temperamental steed. A horse with a little age on him would be more satisfactory.

A horse over eight years of age is probably the best buy. From eight on, a horse has become set in his ways and is usually mellowed enough to take things casually, and consequently will not go all to pieces when you begin acting in an unorthodox manner on his back. Unusual sights and sounds will not spoil his stride. Generally he will approach the matter of trick riding in a sober, interested frame of mind. He has outgrown his playful colthood and is now old enough to use his head in case of an emergency.

The conformation of the horse is of considerable importance. The ideal height for trick riding is around fifteen hands for adults, or whatever height sets the horse's withers about level with the shoulders of the rider.

A crested or flabby neck is a handicap as it is difficult to balance on a wobbling, bobbing neck. Get a horse with a solid, well-built neck which does not rise too abruptly from the withers.

7

Many tricks are done off the rump of the horse and into the saddle or onto the neck. If the horse has a long back, the rider must travel a long way to reach his destination. A short-coupled horse makes rear tricks easier and is also an easier type to keep fat and sleek. The short-backed horse has a good roll to his canter and consequently provides the rider with a strong lift for vaulting tricks.

As trick riding involves considerable pull on the saddle it is in the interests of safety that a fairly high set of withers is recommended. A little round horse will have to be cinched into the saddle until he bulges to prevent the saddle from turning.

The withers should help to hold the saddle in place and any rider who has found himself unintentionally hanging upside down with the horse's four legs banging him in the head will look for withers before buying another mount.

As your hand runs over the horse's withers, go on back and press a bit on the area over the kidneys. A horse with a painful kidney area can not be used successfully for trick riding as back-of-the-saddle tricks will hurt him and he will object.

It goes without saying that the horse should be free of the standard blemishes such as ringbone, spavin, roaring, poor vision, etc.

There are certain qualities which make up *the ideal trick riding horse. He is fitted by temperament and conformation to be used in the proper presentation of the greatest number of different stunts.* As for color, sex, and breeding, that is a matter of individual preference. Some prefer one, some prefer another, and all can become quite loud in defense of their choice.

Actually there are no mystic qualities connected with color. There have been elaborate stories written to prove that sorrel horses are temperamental, that palominos cannot be trusted, that blacks are mean, and that pintos are dumb. None of them has any factual basis. Buy any color of horse that appeals to you and remember that his temperament and conformation are of far greater importance.

Color is only important if you are going into trick riding professionally. For show purposes it is best to have an exciting color and then to select your own clothes to show up well against it.

8

The problem of sex is slightly different. It is well to remember that trick riding is generally done where there are other horses. A stallion is seldom satisfactory as he will exhibit interest beyond the business of running straight. Stallions are a constant problem and are very, very rarely used for trick riding.

Some riders use mares but they, too, can make themselves a definite nuisance at times. They are often prejudiced against rump tricks and can seldom be trained to accept them completely.

Most riders prefer a gelding and, if you intend to learn all the tricks in this book, you will, too. Only a gelding will stand for many of them.

The breed of the horse does not enter the field at all. The conformation necessary for successful trick riding automatically removes pure-bred horses. A pure Thoroughbred is usually too tall and too long backed. The American Saddlebred has such a thick, heavy neck that stands and vaults to the neck are almost impossible. Arabs are a little light to balance the weight, and the Standardbred tends to be too highly strung and nervous.

Mixtures of these breeds are often good. The Quarter Horse and Morgan are good. Generally speaking the breed is of no importance, so any cold blood having the desired conformation will do. Trick riding is, after all, a western sport, in no way concerned with stud books or registration papers.

## 3. TRAINING THE TRICK-RIDING HORSE

IT IS NOT ENTIRELY NECESSARY to train a horse for trick riding since experienced riders have elected to stunt on everything from bucking horses to a Missouri mule. In its normal aspects, however, trick riding involves some kind of mutual agreement between horse and rider. Most feel it is a decided asset if the horse has decided to be co-operative.

It is also a good thing, when you are learning, to have at least one of you know what you are doing. As the horse has the easiest part it is convenient to teach him first. And, as the simple training of the horse will involve certain variations from the normal position in the saddle, it also helps the rider.

Briefly, the horse is to run straight, at an even, fast gait, without stopping until he has reached the end of the run or "station". He cannot run with complete, gay abandon as to some extent he must be watching with more than mere curiosity for the trick that is coming up. He can then shift and balance his own weight to counteract the off-center weight of the rider.

Training might begin unglamorously with the horse tied to a post. If there is any doubt about the horse's disposition this is a good way to start. Resurrect an old grain sack, shake the dust out and rub it over the horse, but all over. Now begin gently tossing the sack over his back and rump. Throw it around his shoulders and his legs, and if none of this bothers him, throw it across his neck. Keep this up until the horse is thoroughly bored with you. Throw the sack between his legs, under his belly, in every possible place until he proves he isn't spooky.

Work slowly and gently, gradually getting the horse accustomed to being touched. For in trick riding your body will at some time or other be in all the places where that sack has been. If the horse will not stand for the sack, he certainly is not going to stand for you.

Do not at any time try to force the horse to accept this treatment and above all do not lose your temper if he learns slowly. The process involves teaching the horse that these strange objects will not hurt him. Let him take his time to find this out. When he shows no reaction whatever to the treatment, you are ready to ride him.

Training from here on is done in full equipment. We are assuming of course that the horse is not a raw colt, but is already well broken to the saddle.

Full equipment is used because the standard trick-riding saddle is a little longer than the average saddle and is equipped with a double rigging. Even a horse perfectly trained to normal equipment may consider that this outfit smacks of a flank strap and be annoyed. He may wish to dispose of the whole business. Ride him about naturally until he has accepted the situation and pays no more attention to it.

To follow up this acceptance, slide back of the saddle cautiously. Try this first while the horse is standing still. Keep a firm grip on the reins with one hand and on the horn with the other. Now slide behind the saddle and, if the horse acts as if he wants to buck, jerk up a little on the reins and return to the saddle quickly. Usually it only takes a few minutes for the horse to become accustomed to a weight on his rump instead of in the saddle. Don't rush him.

When the horse is completely bored with the whole business it is probably safe to slide all the way to the ground from his rump. Caution! Keep your feet away from his flanks at all times and land free of him with as little jolt as possible. If you keep quiet, he will too.

After a number of tries at sliding off the rump when the horse is at a standstill, try it at a walk. We do not suggest that you slide off at the canter just yet since you might lose your mount. Have someone ride in the saddle at the walk while you are riding double and blithely jumping off his rear. If he pays no attention you can try jumping back on from the rear too. If he seems to be merely tolerating this it is best to run ahead and remount via the stirrup each time. Do not force him on this issue as he has the advantage if an argument should arise.

Continuous work off the rear will soon give an idea of what to expect and, discovering that it is not painful or frightening, he will accept it. Now he can be worked at a canter, riding double until he proves trustworthy. Next, go back to working at a standstill. Start crawling all over the horse. Sit on his neck, stand in the stirrup on both sides, reach under his neck, under his stomach, stand in the saddle, stand behind the saddle, sit backwards, swing your weight a little in each position. Your horse will assume you have lost your mind, he may be concerned over your condition at first, and then he will accept it. You have obviously lost your mind, but it's kind of fun.

Now is the time to start working at the canter in an appropriate place. By appropriate we mean a track, dirt road, or arena large enough for a good long run, and uncomplicated by stakes, poles, ruts, and fences.

You need a place with some type of boundary which the horse can see and use to plan his run. The footing should be smooth and soft so that the horse will not stumble or hurt his legs and you will not sprain an ankle or shove your spinal column up between your ears.

Whenever practical, work the horse away from the stable, for distractions will only prolong the training.

It is best to work the horse from one closed gate to the other rather than to attempt teaching him to go past an opening he has already used as entrance or exit. Work him in approximately the middle of the arena for he must not get into the habit of running close to the fences where the momentum of a vault could easily wrap you around it like a coat of paint.

Start educating the horse at the walk and keep him going straight while you wander all over him. At the walk he won't have turned far off the course before you are back in the saddle to straighten him out. Your mount is definitely a creature of habits as illustrated, in the almost forgotten past, by the milk wagon horse who made his door-to-door stops without any guidance from the driver. The habit of going straight without any signal from the rider and condoning the rider's gymnastics is easier and more quickly attained at the walk.

Never underestimate the walking training, for besides being of great benefit to the horse, it is also of great benefit to you. To accustom the horse to your insane antics you must go through all the various tricks and in so doing you are conditioning and training yourself.

When the horse has the idea of going straight from station to station at the walk, it is time to try it at the canter.

Ride at a smooth, fast gait back and forth several times where you have been walking. When you get to the end, stop the horse with a pull on the reins. Try to make this the only time that it is necessary for you to touch the reins. When you get to the end, turn him to the left and start again. Always work at a walk, canter, or run as the trot is an almost useless gait in trick riding.

Now that the horse knows where he is supposed to go and will take the run perfectly with the reins hanging loose on his neck, he is ready for further training. Shift your weight a little to the left as he runs, putting whatever pressure on the reins is necessary to keep him running straight. His natural inclination will be either to stop in confusion or to turn to the left, following your weight as a cue. Keep him running and keep him straight. Work in this manner on both sides, swinging your weight from side to side until he will run straight and true without hesitation.

Even when the horse has apparently mastered this much of his training, when you start to dismount he may stop abruptly to find out what is going on. Keep your left foot in the stirrup, left hand on the horn, start to dismount in the normal way but stop in a standing position on the horse's side, holding the cantle with your right hand.

Keep the horse running with your toe in his side, chirping, yelling insulting names; use whatever method you like, but keep him going. It will only take a few runs to give him the idea. Then work on the right side in the same manner.

The next step requires a little more riding ability on your part for you must begin to climb around on the saddle as you did at the standstill and the walk. When your horse will run with the determination of a freight train, whether you are on his neck, backwards in the saddle, on the rump standing on the right or left side, you are ready to begin trick riding.

This cannot be taught in one lesson as the horse would collapse from exhaustion after dashing back and forth so many times, but often it does not require more than a week to train a trick-riding horse. Sometimes, however, it may take a month. There is some variation in horses at this point. To prolong the training periods do two-thirds of it at a walk. The horse can be "cooled out" after each three runs and the schooling at the walk resumed during this time.

From these exercises, the horse already has a fair idea of how to use his own weight to balance against the rider's. He knows that he must balance himself when you are on the rump, pull when you are on the neck, lean to the opposite direction when you are on the side, and, through it all, keep the same speed. He is practically a master in his field. Now all he needs is to learn to maintain this admirable performance when there are other horses in the arena, when bands are playing, and a crowd is doing its best to scare him.

Should eagerness and enthusiasm make you restless, we can only remind you that tricks can be practiced to a considerable extent at the standstill. The horse will not mind, and it will do you a great deal of good to have the motions definitely in mind before doing them on a running horse in limited space.

To begin riding on a half-trained horse might end in catastrophe unless you are already an expert trick rider. You must remember that the trick-riding horse runs on his own merry way, uninhibited by reins or any other kind of control from the rider. You have no chance to stop him, straighten him, or turn him, once you are doing a trick. In other words, while you are performing, you are only a passenger and must rely on the judgment and training of your mount.

If you start to ride when the horse is still uncertain as to what is expected of him, he may do any number of things which leave you in an ungraceful position on the track. If he has grasped the idea that he is free to indulge in any whim of distraction, and has not yet fully recognized his responsibilty in the performance, he is still as dangerous as an untrained horse.

Train him well before beginning and then confine your first tricks to those that are easily terminated either in the saddle or on the ground. In other words, although strap tricks are the easiest of all the tricks to do, they are dangerous because you cannot fall clear. It is quite discouraging to find yourself hanging by one foot or one arm from a runaway horse.

Each rider has his own talents and special abilities and so some variation is expected; but on the whole be careful of tricks that tie you to the horse until both of you are quite sure of each other.

We have a lot of tricks for you to try. Pick out the ones you like and learn them progressively. Start with the easy ones and build up your confidence, your ability, and your fun.

## 4. SADDLERY, HANDHOLDS, AND GADGETS

TRICK RIDING CAN BE DONE ON ANY KIND OF SADDLE. It can be done with a surcingle. Just a rope will do. Or you can go native like Smokey Chism and do your trick riding on a bareback horse without a strap of leather of any kind.

However, the number of tricks you can do will depend to a large extent upon the saddle you use. Trick riders have now evolved a saddle which allows enough variation in handholds to accomplish any imaginable trick. For this reason the standard trick-riding saddle as manufactured by Porter, Veach, Rowell, Hamley and similar saddle outfits is recommended.

These saddles have a higher than average horn, a low cantle, and crupper holds on the back. Aside from this, the trick-riding saddle looks like a regular western-type roping saddle. It has double rigging which means two girths. It is a little longer than the other western saddles. But it is not conspicuously different and can be decorated with silver, plastic, quilting, or stamping.

Although the saddle will come with the crupper handholds, other holds must be ordered especially or put on after you have the saddle and need them. Holds can easily be ordered from the company are the Hippodrome strap, a Drag strap, Pick-up strap, and Under-the-Belly slings. These holds are used so frequently that they are necessary before you can even begin.

## HIPPODROME STRAP

This is a strap about two inches wide which goes over the seat of the saddle and is fastened to the front rigging rings. It is adjusted to allow just enough room for the insertion of the rider's feet.

The tighter it is over the feet, the better for both balance and safety. When having the strap attached, order a piece of leather two inches wide and about forty inches long. Approximately six inches is doubled back through the rigging ring at each end and is laced in place.

15

## DRAG STRAP

Use a one-and-a-quarter-inch hame strap twenty-four inches in length and buckle it to the forward part of the cinch ring on the right side of the saddle. As this strap is generally used for the various types of foot drags it will be more comfortable if it is all covered with woolskin with the exception of the tip going through the buckle. It should be adjusted so that the foot can easily go through it, but tight enough that the foot will not slip out when doing the trick.

## PICK-UP STRAP

This strap is similar to the drag strap and made in the same way, although seldom covered with sheepskin. It should be fitted with a buckle as you will want to remove it when not actually using it. As it buckles through the saddle fork it is in the way for most tricks.

## UNDER-THE-BELLY SLINGS

Two slings are usually fastened to the right side of the saddle, one above the other. They are used when the rider crosses under his horse's belly from the left side, underneath, to crawl up the right side.

These are fastened to the front and back rigging rings and differ from each other in length. The larger sling should be lined with a round steel rod so that there will be no sag or stretching of the strap as it is grasped. A sag will drop the rider about two inches as he pulls himself from under the horse. Two inches may be insignificant when you are driving across the State of Texas, but, when you are hanging underneath a running horse, every inch counts.

## BREAST COLLAR AND BLINKERS

These have no relationship to each other except that some riders use them and some don't. And you, too, may use them or not, just as you wish.

The breast collar helps to hold the saddle in place and the stirrup can be tied to it as an aid when going under the horse's neck. It can be used as a handhold for some other tricks too, if you find it handy. Actually its purpose is to prevent the saddle from sliding back and if you do a great many crupper vaults it is almost necessary.

Blinkers are used if the horse tends to duck objects flying close to his head. The "objects" which will be flying around the horse's head will be yourself. Splits to the neck and reverse cruppers to the neck are almost always better done if the horse does not feel it is necessary to dodge flying legs.

Aside from this rather standard equipment, nothing else is really necessary for successful trick riding. You may find that you want to put on extra handholds later, but these will take care of almost every known trick.

Unusual gadgets, specialized holds and other unique riggings, will be found completely described later on in this book in the full instructions for doing each of these fantastic creations.

**THE SADDLE TREE**
1—Ground Seat
2—Gullet
3—Bars
4—Rigging

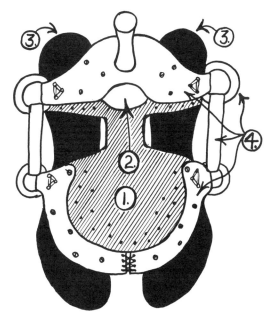

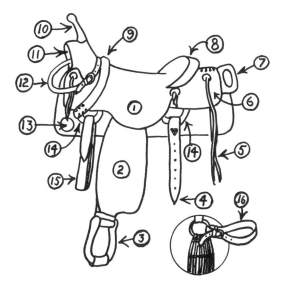

1—Side Jockey
2—Fender
3—Stirrup
4—Billet
5—Strings
6—Back Jockey
7—Crupper Handholds
8—Cantle
9—Hippodrome Strap
10—Horn
11—Fork
12—Pick Up Strap
13—Shoulderstand Handhold
14—Rigging Rings
15—Latigo
16—Drag Strap

## 5. IT'S EASY! IT'S HARD! IT'S DIFFICULT! IT'S SUICIDAL!

TODAY IT IS SAFE TO SAY that more than 142 different tricks or variations can be done by one man on one horse.

In this listing we use the term variations but we list them individually, for if a rider knows one and can do it well it does not mean that he can do the other.

For instance, all trick riders worthy of the name do a vault and split to the horse's neck but how many of today's hundreds of trick riders land *forward* on the horse's neck instead of assuming the regulation backward position?

The following list does not pretend to sum up all the stunts possible; but it is offered as an incomplete descriptive catalog of tricks that *have* been accomplished and performed in shows at one time or another.

Dick Griffith claims there is no limit to what can be done on a slow cantering horse. We could add to this. Many trick riders learn to do their routines when the horse is going slow and are then able to do them successfully on a fast-running mount. The greatest difficulty is the intestinal fortitude it requires to do this and Dick as a champion had the "guts" to do even the hardest tricks on horses that were practically running away.

It is quite difficult to label the different tricks since the sport has never been studied or chronicled sufficiently to provide standard names for the movements, positions, or attitudes. Other trick sportsmen, divers, trapeze performers, hand balancers, swimmers and even airplane pilots have standard appellations for their acrobatic maneuvers. Perhaps in time a simple series of names will be adopted for all of the trick rider's accomplishments.

A RATING DENOTING THE DIFFICULTY OF TRICK RIDING STUNTS.

*5 POINT TRICKS* (13)

1—The Horn Spin
4—The Half Lazyback
16—Crouch Stand From a Strap
19—Half Fender Drag
21—Forward Fender Drag
28—Hippodrome Stand
31—Hippodrome Stand Back of the Cantle
32—The Jack Wright Drag
33—Stirrup over the Horn Drag
34—Indian Squat

18

19

# PART TWO:
# TRICK RIDING

## 6. TRICK RIDING: 144 WAYS TO BREAK YOUR NECK

BEFORE BEGINNING, a few suggestions will be appropriate. First it must be understood that all tricks with few exceptions are started at the run with the rider sitting in a normal position in the saddle. The trick is done and when the horse reaches the "station" the rider should be back in position and in control of the horse.

1. Always check your saddle before starting. See that it is properly cinched and that the holds are in good condition. Nothing will spoil your form so completely as an upside down saddle or a broken handhold.

2. Always work your horse down the center of the track or arena. This will keep him in proper training and will avoid the unpleasantness of cracking your ankles against a fence post.

3. Never practice alone. If something goes wrong you may need help, and when you need help in trick riding you need it quickly.

4. Always turn your horse to the left when starting from the station. This will put him on a left lead in which both the front and back legs go forward at the same time. As trick riding is done on the left lead it is important that the horse always take it. If turned to the right he may take a right lead, or worse yet, be on a right lead in front and a left lead behind which is much too rough for trick riding.

5. Uncinch your horse when you have finished and let him know with a few pats on the neck or a carrot that he did well.

There are several tricks which are good for beginning and you may select whichever one appeals to you the most. One of the easiest requires a bit of balance and is known as the Sprinter's Crouch. The most valuable for future work is the Single Vault. And the most awkward is the Spin Around the Horn. You will have to learn this last one soon. It is a good trick when done with grace and assurance but in the beginning—you might as well accept it—you will look like a three-armed madman.

Practice these three tricks as a foundation and then you are ready to start seriously. Seriously means that you will work on each trick until it is done with ease, assurance, and with at least some degree of grace. There are certain devices which may seem foolish but which will assist you in the achievement of these qualities.

First, never look down at the ground. If you do so, to the audience you will appear timid and, as a matter of fact, a serious consideration of the earth rushing by beneath you is very likely to cause you some qualms.

When doing top tricks watch either the horse's head or, if you are facing backward, his rump, as an aid in maintaining your balance. If you select a point on the horizon to study you will be inclined to follow that direction instead of the direction which the horse is taking. And then you will lose your balance.

Swing into tricks with rhythm and in time with the motion of the horse. A cantering horse has a definite rocking motion which should be used to your advantage. If you go against the natural rhythm of the horse you may be thrown off balance and certainly the tricks will be more difficult.

With these points in mind, study the following photographs and descriptions and try to duplicate them as nearly as possible. Anyone with average strength, balance, and rhythm should be able to do at least 20 of the first 30 tricks. Take your time, fool around with them, and you will see how simple they are. When done according to instruction the tricks are safer, so pay attention. No matter how fantastic the tricks which experts do, they observe the motto: "Live dangerously but safely".

If your balance is especially good you may find top tricks easier than the other types. The person with good timing and spring will find that vaults are a cinch whereas others will find them difficult. Such variations are to be expected and you should train yourself accordingly. You should also keep in mind the eventual outlet of your trick riding.

If your trick riding is to be used in rodeo work, anything goes. You have plenty of room and a good runway clear of obstacles, and so have opportunity to do all tricks.

If circus work is your aim, remember that it is often difficult to do a complicated routine because tricks must be timed to avoid stakes and quarter poles. Circuses have short tracks, usually only 130 feet long, and so you should select tricks that are fast to get into and out of. Find tricks that can maintain their action at the center of the grandstand but find you back in the saddle in a few seconds. Combination runs are almost impossible in a circus tent.

Fairs often place the trick rider on the race track which means a very long run before the grandstand. Any trick which can be held for a long run is good for fairs. The Russian Drag, Fender Drag, Stroud Layout, Cossack Stand, Slick Saddle Stand, Shoulder Stand, etc., are all suitable. If your endurance is good, the vaults are fine, but ten double vaults will exhaust the average rider. Here the combination runs are ideal for perhaps four tricks could be done in rapid sequence during each run.

Should your trick riding be aimed at foundation for gymkhana games, concentrate on the vaults, pick-ups, scissors in the saddle both front and back, and flying mounts.

And if you want to trickride just for your own amusement and amazement, start logically, perfecting especially basic tricks such as the vaults. Learn everything. When you have learned to do every trick in this book you can start inventing your own. You will then be the most terrific rider in the business. Go to it!

Byron Hendricks perched birdlike over his two bridleless bareback horses while executing his original breath-taking Roman ride over a four-foot bar obstacle.

25

1

## THE TWO-HANDED HORN SPIN

At first this trick is a tortured crawl from the saddle to the neck and back into the saddle. You will get immense satisfaction from having done it, but those watching you may not be impressed with its artistic value. Before starting, dispose of the reins. Run them through the throat latch or tuck them beneath the crown of the bridle, but get them away somewhere.

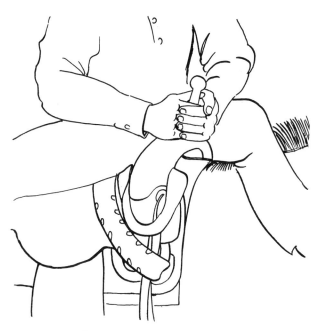

**The Two Hand Horn Spin**

**Buck Eddy doing a Horn Spin to Backward on the Neck**

Start the horse going. Keep the left foot in the stirrup, swing the right leg across the horse's neck. Kick the left foot out of the stirrup and make a quick shift, pivoting with your hands on the saddle horn, until you are astride the neck. Now place the right leg across the saddle and pivot in the same way into the saddle.

Practice this until you can make it almost one continuous pivot, and swing around and around the horn, from saddle to neck to saddle again. It is not a difficult trick, and, even if you should fall, you always have a hold on the horn and can therefore vault back onto the horse. You will not be hurt and actually you will be doing another trick. Every recovered fall is a trick!

←≪ **START**

27

# ONE-HAND HORN SPIN

To make a more difficult trick from the simple process of turning onto the neck and back into the saddle, do it with one hand and raise the other high above your head.

**Bernice Dean doing One Hand Horn Spin**

A good build-up to this one-handed method is to practice with your left hand on the top of the horn, throw your right leg onto the neck and then, only when necessary, use the right hand to grab the mane for balance and any pull that is needed to accomplish the swing; when returning to the saddle, use your right hand on the cantle only when you have to. With a little practice you will develop a way of leaning on the left hand with sufficient strength to pivot your entire body around it without using the right hand as an aid. Gradually

← START

depend less and less upon the right hand and with a few tries you will be able to accomplish the horn spin with your right hand held well above your head.

Now start your horse and try it on the run. Practice this three or four times a day and by the end of the week you can invite your chums over to see it.

# FREE HORNSPIN, or NO HANDS HORNSPIN

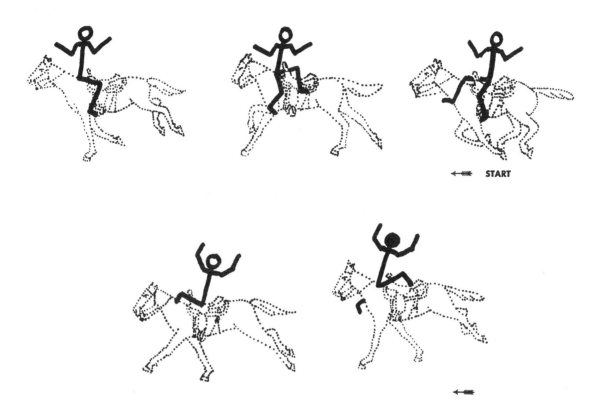

This is a tricky variation credited to Ted Elder who, if not really the originator, was certainly capable of dreaming up this teaser.

Like all the "free" accomplishments, this one has a definite "perhaps you do and perhaps you don't" element that may take a great deal of practice to overcome. The greatest aid, of course, is to follow up the successful execution of the two preceding tricks with a lot of no hands horn-spinning practice while your horse is walking. Learn to shift your weight to be balanced at all times, for skill rather than brute strength provides the keynote to keeping you atop the horse. Of course, if you start to fall you can grasp the horn to recover your balance.

**The "Free Hornspin" demonstrated by Dick Borello**

# 4
## ONE FOOT LAYOVER THE SADDLE

For many riders the One Foot Layover the Saddle is easier than the Lay Down although they are very similar. Start the horse going, swing your right leg over the horn and into the saddle. Take the left crupper hold with your left hand and the horn with your right hand.

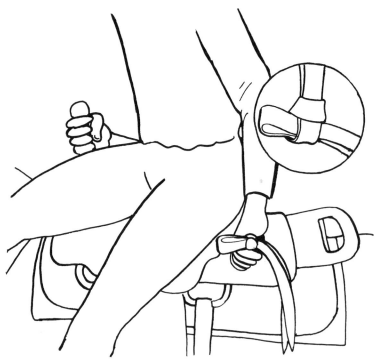

**The Layover Handholds**

Keep the left foot in the stirrup and bend backward until you are lying across the saddle. Now raise the right leg high into the air, to a position perpendicular to the horse. This is an extremely flashy trick and looks especially good if the toe is pointed and the body held close to the horse.

To get out of the trick simply sit up again, release the hand holds and swing the right leg back into normal riding position.

Because the trick can be so rapidly finished, it can be held for almost the entire run, giving the audience an opportunity to appreciate

**Bernice Dean doing a One Foot Lay Over the Saddle**

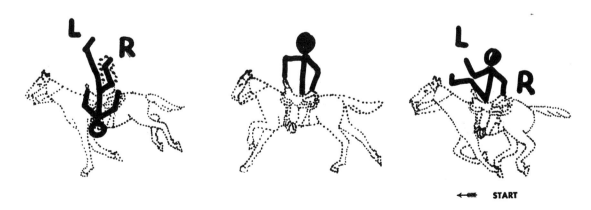

START

# 5
## LAZY BACK

Done properly this is as easy as lying on a couch. Done improperly it will knock the wind out of you. Start your horse and swing your right leg over to the left side so that you are sitting sideways in the saddle.

Take the left crupper handhold or saddle string with your left hand and the saddlehorn with your right hand. Now slide down the left side of the horse leaning backward at the same time. When the small of your back is across the seat of the saddle, raise both feet to a horizontal position and hold it to the station.

To come back into the saddle, lower the feet and work your way back into the saddle. Lift your right leg over the horn and you will be back in riding position. Be careful in this not to come up before you have shifted your balance in the saddle. You might keep right on going forward.

Practice at a standstill several times until you have the feel of the trick. It is not a sign of timidity to ask someone to lead your horse at a walk so that you can find the best place to balance yourself while moving. When you feel secure in the trick, do it on the run.

**Pee Wee Burge doing a Layover in the Saddle**

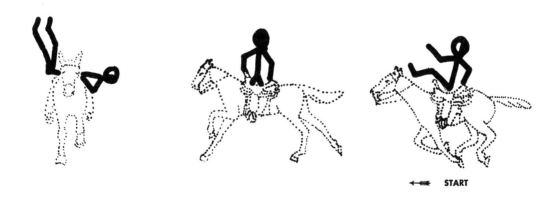

← START

35

# FREE LAZYBACK

In 1912 Bee Hoo Gray decided to experiment with the idea of doing a free lie down in the saddle. By "free" he meant doing it with both hands and feet dangling out in space, using no holds of any kind. The trick was a success. It has been copied by most trick riders who have a good sense of balance. Those who do not trust their balance should not attempt it.

It is usually a good idea to practice this trick several times at a standstill to get the feel of it and find your point of balance.

Swing to a sideways position in the saddle catching the crupper hold with your left hand and the horn with your right hand. Slide a little forward so that, as you lie down across the horse, the small of your back will be on the saddle. When you feel well balanced, release your hold on the crupper and horn, kick your left foot free of the stirrup and stretch out straight across the saddle.

The point is to balance on your back just as a pencil can be balanced across a finger. Because of the motion of the horse, it takes a little time to find just the position that will hold. When learning, it is intelligent to practice with your hands strategically placed to catch the horn and crupper holds quickly.

Most riders tend to keep the center of balance slightly tipped toward the feet as from this position a fall can be converted easily into a vault back to the saddle. If you fall in the other direction you will land on your head.

To get out of the trick you can swing up to a sitting position, catch the horn with both hands, drop to the ground, and vault into the saddle. Or you can stop in the sitting position and, by using both handholds for balance, throw your leg over the horn into the normal riding position.

Bee Hoo Gray, the originator of this riding stunt was better known for his great trick-roping ability. He won many trick-roping championships and for many years performed his popular roping act at theatres, night clubs, and fairs continuing this until his death in Pueblo, Colorado, on August 3rd, 1951.

← START

**The Free Lazyback. Both of Dick Borello's hands are in the air, though one is hidden behind the horse's mane.**

# 7
## LAZYBACK ROLL BACK

The Cossacks attributed the origin of this trick to a famous White General who was a fearless trick rider.

The feat is done from the sideways position of the Lazyback as explained in No. 5 but in this difficult version the rider goes completely over backward until his feet touch the ground. He hangs here in a doubled up position from the side of his horse and kicks the ground with his feet to secure the aid of the lift for his return to the saddle.

Don't make the mistake others have made and consider this an easy accomplishment. If you do you may find yourself still hanging from your horse in the doubled up position when he reaches the station. Practice at the standstill or walk until you are sure of it.

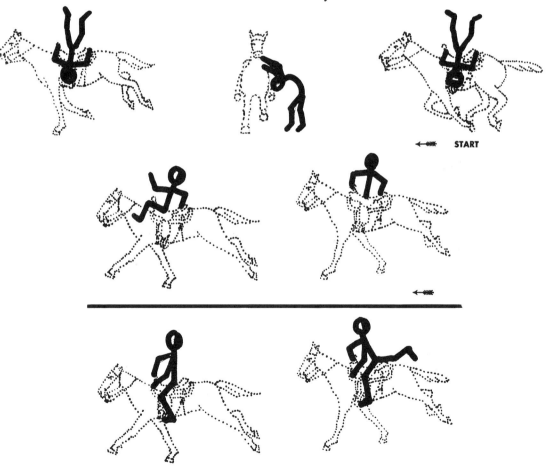

38

# HALF UPSIDE DOWN ON THE NECK

This is another of the really easy beginner's tricks that can be quickly learned.

To start, grasp the horn and mane and raise the left leg to the rear over the saddle to the right side. Stand in the right stirrup (on the right leg) turn the left hand to a thumb down grip on the horn and lean forward to bend head downward over the neck of the horse. As you bend with your stomach against the horse's neck the right hand secures a grip either on the breast collar or shoulder stand handhold on the left of the saddle. The free foot (the left) is raised perpendicular above the rider to complete the trick.

To return to the saddle, the left foot is lowered, to cross the saddle as the rider straightens up to the normal riding position.

Some riders grasp the saddle horn with the left hand held upside down at the start instead of making the change as explained above.

**Bernice Dean doing a Half Upside Down on the Neck**

← START

# UPSIDE DOWN ON THE NECK

This is done just a little differently than the preceeding trick and results in a better, more finished-looking position.

The rider goes into the trick from the standing position on the right side of the horse as in No. 8 but has the right hand in the shoulderstand handhold in the right front skirt corner of his saddle. The left hand is upside down gripping the horn as the rider leans over the neck of the horse and raises both feet up to a vertical position.

When performing any trick requiring both feet to be held in a horizontal or vertical position, always remember to keep the legs together and point the toes. Nothing detracts as much from a graceful appearance as spread legs and clumsily placed feet. Many riders, conscious of this fact, cross their legs to attain a more pleasing appearance.

This trick is often used in combination with the Pinwheel Cartwheels described in No. 67.

To combine these two the rider lets go with his right hand, while he is upright in the Upside Down on the Neck, and grasps the saddle horn with it as he falls forward into the Pinwheel Cartwheels.

The combination runs really show the skill of the rider. Whenever possible, combine as many tricks as you can perform smoothly in the length of the run.

The more easily you can go from trick to trick, the greater the number that can be done in sequence. It may be impossible in the beginning for you to do more than two tricks during one run. Later, however, after much practice, you will find it is possible to add and complete more and still more of these combinations in the same distance.

To return to the saddle the rider spreads his legs as he lowers them and twists his body as he rises to land astride the saddle.

One of our champions, Ken Williams, did a Vault to Backwards in the Saddle to a Tailstand to a Scissors to the Saddle to a Hornspin to Neck Scissors to a Single Vault all in one run; accomplishing this entire routine in approximately 200 feet! He did it as smoothly as flowing oil with not one split second of waste motion—truly a masterpiece of riding ability.

← START

Frank Dean doing an Upside Down on the Neck

41

## LAYOVER THE NECK

The ease with which this trick, and others on the neck, are done depends somewhat upon the horse. If the horse has a long, solid neck with a good mane, it is quite simple. Should your horse's neck have a large wobbling muscle forming the crest you will have to adjust your position to compensate for the movement.

Grasp the saddle horn in your right hand. Keeping the right foot in the stirrup, step out of the saddle to the right and roll forward onto the neck, turning onto your back on the neck, catching the mane in your left hand as a handhold. As soon as you feel secure, raise your left foot into the air as nearly perpendicular as possible. The right foot remains in the stirrup all through this trick.

To return to the saddle, straighten up and pivot on the right stirrup back into the saddle. If this is done in a smooth, wide swing it will be part of the trick instead of merely an anticlimatic end.

Practice at a standstill and at a walk before going into motion. The trick depends greatly upon the swing onto the neck and back into the saddle. A little practice will give you an idea of the timing and make the trick easy. This is another trick quite popular with the cowgirl trick riders.

**Chickie Eddy doing a Lay Over the Neck**

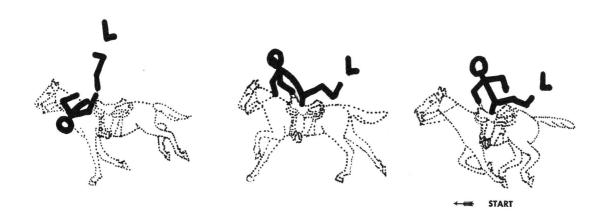

START

43

# LAY OVER THE NECK TO VAULTS

This is quite similar to the preceeding trick but requires a bit more agility and balance. After getting into the Lay Over the Neck the rider turns loose the mane to grasp the horn with both hands, kicks the right foot out of the stirrup, and raises it alongside the left. The rider balances on the neck in this position for a few moments and then rolls backward to hit the ground with his feet for a single vault back into the saddle.

**Chuck Chism doing a Lay Over the Neck with both feet in the air**

When used in combination this way as an outlet for tricks, riders often forego the above described method and roll into the Lay Over the Neck directly from the two hands on the saddlehorn position.

← START

Sitting forward in the saddle, the rider grasps the saddlehorn with both hands, steps off to the right, turns to lie back across the horse's neck, and raises both feet in the air. The feet should be held together, the toes pointed, while in this position, to prevent an awkward, clumsy look. Too often lack of rhythm and grace spoil what would otherwise be a skilfully done trick.

**"Doc" Docsteader doing a Lay Over the Neck to Vaults**

## SPRINTER'S CROUCH STAND IN THE SADDLE

This is a neat trick, easily done, good for exhibition, and ideal for combining with the Saddle Somersault No. 65 or Spread-eagle Cartwheels No. 68.

Put your left hand in the left crupper handhold or grasp the rear saddlestring and place your right hand, thumb down, on the horn. Throw your weight onto the right stirrup to make it easy to draw your left leg up beneath you where you put the foot in the saddle seat. Now stand on that one leg as straight as possible and raise the right leg into the air.

It is wise to go into this slowly to guard your balance, as a fast rise may throw you forward and once you lose your balance it is very difficult to regain from this position. Your brace from the arms is largely for the forward and backward motion of the horse and you must compensate for any sideward throw with balance alone.

To return to the saddle, let the left leg slip off the saddle seat and at the same time lower the right leg. You will automatically fall into the saddle.

If during the trick you lose your balance beyond the point of recovery and fall forward, you will be in the same position as at the beginning of this and the saddle somersault combination. Don't worry, but finish the trick as described in No. 65 or No. 68.

**Sprinter's Stance or Crouch Stand in the Saddle as done by Ken Maynard**

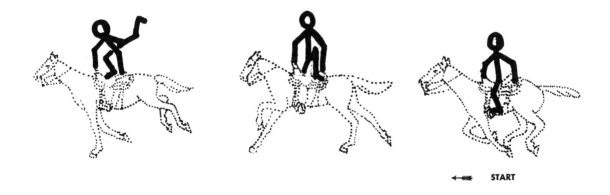

← START

47

## SPRINTER'S CROUCH ON THE RUMP

The rider pushes over the cantle to ride back of the saddle, grasps the extreme ends of the cantle with both hands, rises to his knees, then lifts the left leg to a stand on the left foot, and raises the right leg high overhead. Both legs and arms are kept as straight as possible while the position is held. To return to the saddle it is an easy matter

**Bernice Dean doing a Crouch Stand on the Rump**

to drop down astride the horse, grasp the saddlehorn, and pull yourself back over the cantle to the normal position.

After a reasonable amount of trick-riding practice, your co-
ordination with the motion of the horse will allow you to take advantage of his up-and-down motion, or lift, to simplify passing back
and forth over the cantle. The hands are pressed against the saddle
or rump and the body pushed into the air, leap-frog-like, on the upward movement of the horse. With this push, it is possible to go ahead
or back by leaning or throwing one's weight in the direction desired.

←◀◀◀ **START**

14

## BACKWARD SPRINTER'S STANCE

Some tricks are complicated by requiring a combination of ac-
tivities. This is one of them. The rider must turn around backward
in the saddle, do the stand, and then turn around facing forward
again before reaching the station. For obvious reasons it is wise to
practice fast turns in the saddle (Saddle Spins No. 36) before going
on with the stand part of the trick. Should your turn be slow you may
find yourself at the station before ever getting into the real part of
the trick. Or worse yet, you may arrive at the station only half way on
the return to normal position.

The fastest way to get into position is through the use of a Saddle
Scissors, No. 38, which is the method used by some riders. The more
conventional manner, however, is to start with the Saddle Spin to get
backward in the saddle.

When you are facing backward, take the crupper holds in both hands, and boost yourself to a crouching position with your feet in the saddle. Like Smokey Chism in the photograph, you will find it helps to brace your sturdier leg against the saddle fork. Now raise the other foot high into the air. Hold that pose for as long as possible, but allow sufficient time for the return to a forward sitting position in the saddle.

This Backward Sprinter's Crouch can be quite effectively combined with the Billy Keen Drag No. 94. The rider dives out of this crouch, over the tail, to fall into the drag.

**Smokey Chism doing a Backward Crouch Stand in the Saddle**

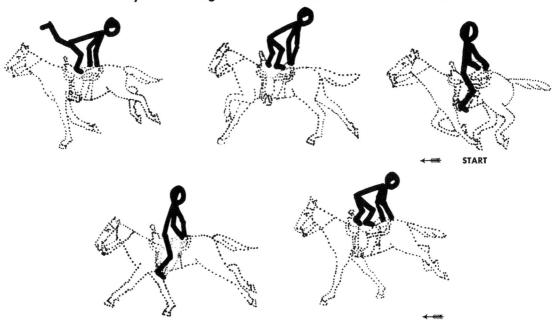

START

## SPRINTER'S STANCE ON THE NECK

In learning some tricks you might as well accept the idea that you and the horse are very likely to part company a few times before the stunt will be mastered. Any stands done on the neck are closely related to wire walking and must be considered as balancing tricks. If your balance is not especially good, practice it on the ground first. When you feel fairly sure of yourself, start on the horse.

Take the horn with your left hand and put your right foot on the horse's withers just in front of the horn. Now take a good tight hold of the horse's mane with your right hand, the horn with your left, thumb down. Carefully pull yourself up to a standing position keeping the center of balance over your right foot on the withers. Slowly extend your left leg, compensating for its weight by leaning very slightly forward. If you press your foot a little to the right side of the crown of the withers it will give a little brace against a forward fall.

A backward fall from this trick can sometimes be caught by throwing yourself back into the saddle or by catching the horn with the right hand as you go down and converting the fall into a vault.

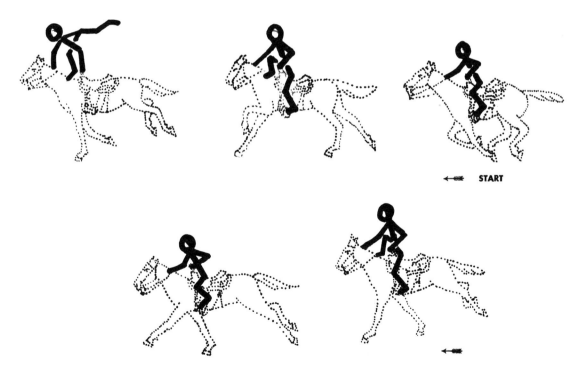

START

### SPRINTER'S STANCE FROM THE WITHERS

This trick looks much more difficult than it actually is. It is, however, a strap trick and so should not be used until you are reasonably sure of your horse and have a smooth track on which to work. All strap tricks in which you are tied to the horse and can not fall free are dangerous.

Slide your left foot into the Hippodrome strap as close as possible to the rigging ring. The strap should come tightly across the instep. Now start your horse with your foot in this position, but with your right hand on the horn, the left on the reins. When he has hit his stride, release the reins and use the left hand on the mane. With a lurch in the general direction of his ears you will find yourself standing on your left foot which is in the strap, and securely held in position by your hands on the mane and saddlehorn. To add flash to the trick extend your right leg back and up.

During the trick you will be facing slightly to the right. To return to the saddle, swing around facing forward, bring your right foot down from its flight and simply sit down. Remove your left foot from the strap and there you are.

It is the forward fall which is difficult to catch, is most frequent, and which leaves the rider with a dusty taste in his mouth.

To get out of the trick simply bring your left foot down, turn to line up with the horse and sit down, bringing your feet with you. Often it is not necessary to release your hold on the mane at all and certainly there is no reason to free the horn until you are again seated in the saddle.

Smokey Chism doing a Sprinter's Stance on the Neck

The Crouch Stand from the Withers as done by Juanita Gray, who was a featured trick rider at Cheyenne Frontier Days for over ten years

← START

## BACKWARD CROUCH STAND FROM THE WITHERS

The Hippodrome strap is used in executing this trick also. It differs from the preceding trick primarily in that it is started from the rider's backward position on the horse's neck. The rider holds the saddlehorn in the left hand while the other lifts the Hippodrome strap for the entrance of the right foot. Releasing the strap, the rider grasps the left side of the cantle and rises into the stand. The legs and arms are kept as straight as possible in this as with all the other Crouch Stand positions. Facing backward, the rider extends the free, raised leg, with the toes pointed forward, out over the horse's head.

**Bernice Dean doing the Backward Crouch Stand**

This trick is ideal to use as a combination followup for the Backward Hippodrome Stand No. 30. The rider does the Hippodrome Stand, then removes one foot to go directly into the Backward Crouch Stand, performing both in a single run.

This was always a pet combination of Bernice Dean who is credited with being the originator of this Backward Crouch Stand.

The two stunts are seldom seen since the rider has to learn to control the horse from an awkward backward position.

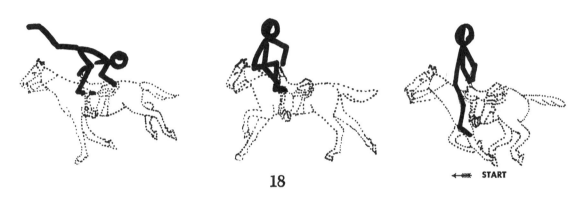

18

← START

## ARABESQUE OR ONE-KNEE STAND

Any trick of this kind is recommended where the run is short. It is quick to get into and out of and still makes a good appearance.

Grasp the fork of the saddle with both hands and push yourself over the cantle until you are sitting back on the horse's rump. Now grasp the cantle or the saddle skirts and raise yourself to your knees. It will help if you raise yourself in rhythm with the horse.

As you get your balance, lift the right leg in the air. If the left leg is placed at a slight angle across the horse's rump, it will help to give you balance. Hold this position the full length of the track.

To get out and back into the saddle, lower your right leg to the kneeling position, slide down straddling the rump. Place your hands on the front of the saddle and swing back into position.

Simple, isn't it? This is one of many tricks which a saddle club could adopt. Trick riding of this type can be done by a whole troop of horsemen in unison. Other clubs might wear pure silver and ride solid gold saddles and not be as unique as a trick-riding club.

Bernice Dean doing an Arabesque
or One Knee Stand
←⟞

The Half Fender Drag done
by Jeanne Abbott
⟝→

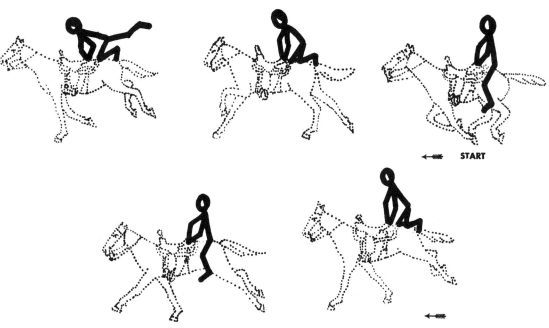

←⟞ START

←⟞

56

## HALF FENDER DRAG

Few of our girl trick riders do a true Fender Drag. Practically all are content with some form of the half-done, one-hand version, relying to a very noticeable extent on their feminine charm which they have found to be an acceptable substitute for their lack of skill.

To do this one-hand, Half Fender Drag, grasp the horn in the left hand, right hand on the cantle. Step off to the left as though to dismount, keeping the left foot in the stirrup. Bend your left knee as you go down and turn to face the rear of the horse. At the same time push the left foot and stirrup out far enough to allow the knee to pass underneath the twisted stirrup leather until it passes across the thigh.

The rider turns loose the right hand, throws it out forward toward the horse's head and extends the free right leg backward, straight out over the toe of the left foot. The body is turned out slightly facing away from the horse and is lowered until at full arm's length from the horn handhold. This completes the so-called Half Fender Drag.

To return to the saddle, the rider reaches up with the right hand to have both hands on the horn, then rises upright in the stirrup to cross the right leg over to resume the normal position in the saddle.

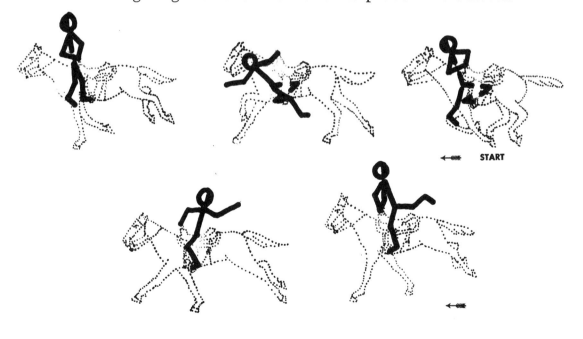

START

## THE FENDER DRAG

It is safe to say that the Fender Drag is one of the most popular tricks ever done in trick riding. Few of the many simple tricks are spectacular or as daring looking.

For many years Montie Montana featured this attractive trick but with an added touch of his own origination. Being a good trick roper, as well as a trick rider, he combined the spinning of a small loop with his rendition of the drag.

**The true Fender Drag as done by Ken Maynard**

The trick is started exactly the same as the preceding one, No. 19. The horn is gripped in the left hand, the rider steps off to the left, squats down facing the saddle and extends the left knee (which is

← START

now in front of the stirrup leather and fender) back between it and the horse as he turns his body to face the rear.

The twisted stirrup leather should be high up on the thigh. The rider crosses the free right leg over the toe of the left foot, extending out of the stirrup and hangs it there to keep it out of the way. Twists outward to face away from the horse, turns loose with both hands and rides the fender leaning over, with hands outstretched.

The position is a secure one since the rider is "locked" up around the stirrup leather when the trick is properly accomplished.

Some trick riders are bothered a bit by the discomfort of riding the twisted stirrup. To overcome this, one of our girl trick riders, Frances Stroud, turns her stirrup around in the opposite direction before doing the trick. At the station right after her preceding run Frances jumps to the ground, checks the tightness of the saddle girth, and remounts. What most observers overlook is the way Frances turns her stirrups when she remounts. This almost unnoticeable movement put her back aboard her horse with the left foot in the stirrup holding the half twist in the stirrup leather. When she steps off into the Fender Drag the leather is flat and not twisted where it crosses her thigh. This provides a little more ease and pleasure to the accomplishment of the drag.

To return to the saddle, the rider raises and twists his body to reach the saddlehorn with his left hand, untwists his locked knee, straightens up, and throws his free leg over the saddle to assume the regular position astride the saddle.

# FORWARD FENDER DRAG

Whereas the standard Fender Drag is done facing the rear of the horse, this Fender Drag is done while facing forward. Note that it is the reverse of the regular Fender Drag and could be so called, but in order to avoid confusion in the names the "Forward" designation was considered advisable.

To do the Forward Fender Drag, step off in the left stirrup facing forward. Bend your left knee to lower yourself, at the same time pushing the stirrup away from the horse. Bring the right leg underneath the stirrup leather, still holding the horn with both hands. With your right knee securely tucked beneath the leather and your weight still on the left leg which is in the stirrup, the leather is held tight.

You can now release the left hand, holding it out to the side. It is wise to keep hold of the horn with your right hand, but straighten the arm so that you appear to be hanging well out from the horse.

A variation of this, which was done by Ted Elder, is to hold the crupper with the right hand, turn with your back to the horse and catch the tail with the left hand. By pulling the tail underneath your left arm you can release the right hand. You will now be doing a straight layout parallel to the horse.

To get out of either trick, simply pull yourself up to a standing position in the stirrup, releasing your leg from beneath the stirrup leather. Swing your right leg over the saddle and there you are.

**The Forward Fender Drag done by Bernice Dean**

# FAYE BLACKSTONE'S FENDER DRAG

This creation of Faye's looks a good deal like the preceding Forward Fender Drag to the casual onlooker. A more careful observation of the trick, however, shows one definite change from the three Fender Drags already described. In this drag the right leg is in the left stirrup!

To start this trick, the rider lifts the right leg over the horn to assume a sideways position in the saddle. The left foot is removed from the stirrup, the right inserted, and, grasping the horn in the left, the crupper hold in the right, the rider squats down alongside the horse. The right knee is against the side of the horse momentarily, then it is pushed forward under the stirrup leather as the rider turns forward. The left handhold is released and the rider hangs down from the outstretched right arm with the left leg extended forward.

To get out of the trick, the rider reaches for the horn and pulls upward to return sideways in the saddle, kicks the foot loose from the stirrup, crosses the right leg over the horn, and is once more in the starting position.

This trick can be combined with others quite easily to make a more interesting run.

Instead of gripping the left crupper handhold the rider holds the right one, when going into the drag. Then, after doing the Blackstone

Fender Drag, the rider drops the left leg to the ground and extends the doubled-up right to drop into the Spread-eagle Drag, No. 98. This the rider does for a short distance, then reaches up and catches the crupper hold with his left hand, kicks the right foot free of the stirrup and is jerked back of the horse in position for a Crupper Jump No. 71. Many of the other crupper or reverse crupper tricks can be used in place of No. 71 if the rider prefers.

**Faye Blackstone's Fender Drag**

## THE COSSACK, RUSSIAN, SUICIDE, OR DEATH DRAG

**Jeanne Abbott doing a Russian Drag in the Saddle**

There is a series of drags from one foot which was adopted, with slight changes, by the cowboys from the Russian Cossacks. They are exciting to watch and, although comparatively easy, are dangerous.

A drag strap is buckled or laced to the cinch ring on the right side and the rider puts his entire foot through the loop so that he hangs by the ankle. He is now tied securely to the horse which enables him to hang free-handed, but also means that he cannot fall free and is at the mercy of his horse.

Do not start any of the Russian drags until you can depend completely upon your horse. Do not start any of the Russian drags unless there is a competent horseman with you in case of trouble. And with a nod of respect to dead trick riders, including one disemboweled Russian, do not do a Russian Drag without first tightening your cinch.

Before starting the horse, put your right foot through the drag loop. Now start your horse and wait until he is well into his stride, as a starting horse can be easily thrown off balance.

When he is going, fall backward off to the left side, at the same time bringing the left foot up forward. Throw your hands free over your head as you go down. You are now dangling by the right foot and hanging upside down with your left foot up in the air. This is one of the most exciting tricks to do but should be performed with confidence and some gay abandon as a timid approach will spoil its appearance.

To return to the saddle bring the left leg down first to the left side. Raise your body by swinging upwards and catching the horn with your left hand to pull yourself up to a sitting position. You now come to the station in complete control of the horse.

The reason for the extra gesture with the left leg is to eliminate the possibility of going completely over the horse into a real suicide drag on the other side. With your left leg already down you are sure of stopping in the saddle. To come up from a drag and go completely over the horse to fall on the right side may mean the end of a trick-riding career if not the end of the trick rider. Any trick where the rider is strapped or tied to his horse is extremely dangerous.

**Ken Maynard, famous Western movie star, shown here doing a Russian Drag Pick-up**

← START

65

## COSSACK DRAG OVER THE NECK

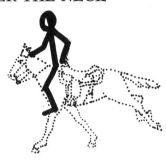

The Russian Cossacks specialized in drags and when they dreamed this one up they definitely threw precaution to the winds. Picture the Cossack blithely sailing off into the air to dangle by one foot against the shoulders of his horse. Remember that he did this in the full military dress of the Czar—and often included a long saber clenched in the teeth.

The American trick rider does the same trick but, having a practical turn of mind, leaves to the Cossack the special joy of impaling himself on his saber.

The trick is started with the right foot in the drag strap, toe in the stirrup. The horse is started and the rider goes forward over the horn to a straddle position on the neck. To do this, hold the mane with the right hand, rest your weight on the toe in the right stirrup. Lift your left leg high enough to reach behind and under it to grasp the horn with the left hand. With these aids boost yourself over the horn and onto the neck.

Now release your hold on the horn. You are in a perfectly normal riding position except that you are sitting astride the neck instead of in the saddle. Don't think the horn will not jab you in the back to remind you of the new position. It will help if the saddle is placed several inches further back than usual when doing this trick, unless your horse comes equipped with a roomy neck.

From this position, twist your body to the right and drop backward to the left side of the horse allowing the left leg to go underneath the neck to rest on the horse's right shoulder point. Release all hand holds and hang free. You will be hanging from your right foot off the left shoulder and a little forward, quite definitely upside down.

To get out of the trick, reach up to grab the horn and pull yourself back onto the neck. From there boost yourself back over the horn and into the saddle.

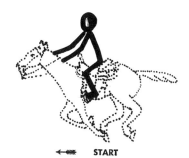

←⋘ START

**The Drag Strap is fastened to the cinch ring**

**Louie Cabral doing a Russian Drag Over the Neck**

## DEATH DRAG BACKWARD OVER THE NECK

This trick is complicated only by the fact that you must make a half horn spin onto the neck before beginning, get your left foot into the drag strap on the right side, do the trick, get out of the strap, and do a half horn spin back into the saddle.

To avoid some of this time-consuming activity many riders begin the run and end it on the neck without attempting to complete all the motions. If you expect to do this, be sure to have someone at the station to catch and stop your horse, for at first you may not be able to control him from this position.

Sit facing backward on the neck. Place your left foot through the drag strap, which is fastened to the cinch ring on the right side. Now bring the right leg up into the air, holding the horn for balance. As the right leg goes up into the air, release your hold on the horn and fall back and to your right. Your arms, head, and the right foot should stand out almost perpendicularly from the shoulders of the horse.

To recover, catch the horn with both hands and, bringing your right leg down on the horse's left side, pull yourself back up on the neck. The proper and safest completion of the trick is to remove the strap from your foot and spin back into the saddle.

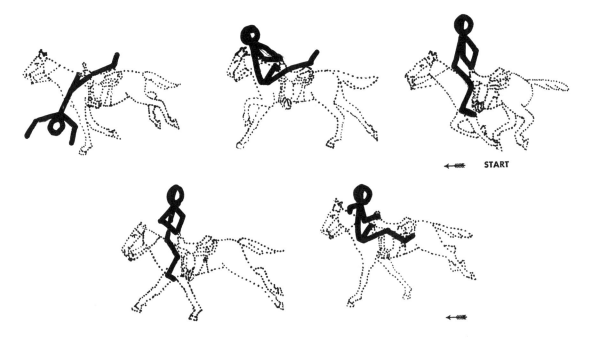

## RUSSIAN DRAG BACK OF THE SADDLE

This variation of the Russian drag is used by long-legged trick riders. It is not usually worth while to use both the drag over the saddle and back of the cantle as they appear to be the same trick from an audience standpoint. But if you are so tall that your head tends to bounce on the ground when dragging across the saddle, use this variation.

Start with your right foot in the drag strap as usual and then boost yourself behind the cantle. From here bring the left foot up in the air and at the same time fall back and away to the left of the horse with the hands reaching in the general direction of the horse's rear hoof.

To recover from this, reach for the saddle strings, cantle, horn, or whatever is handiest for you. Bring your left foot down on the left side of the horse and swing up to a sitting position. Don't pull yourself up with an enthusiastic burst of energy or you may very likely keep on going.

Bring yourself up carefully and clamp tight to the horse with your left leg as this is the only anchor you have to stop the momentum. Should you take this advice lightly you may find yourself doing another kind of drag but this time it will be with your shoulders hitting the ground instead of your finger tips. There is considerable difference.

**Louie Cabral doing a Russian Drag Back of the Saddle**

## THE STROUD LAYOUT

**Leonard Stroud doing his Stroud Layout spinning a rope**

This trick is named after its originator, Leonard Stroud. With what appeared to be the ease of a fly on a wall, he stood on his running horse spinning a rope. But instead of standing on the horse's back with head up and feet down as one usually stands, he stood with his feet on the horse's side with his head off in space. It is not done with suction cup shoes.

**Connie Griffith doing a Stroud Layout**

Use the drag strap but fasten it to the rigging ring on the right side instead of to the cinch ring. When you put your foot through it, your foot will be just off the top on the saddle. Keep your left foot in the stirrup. Now start the horse and hold the horn with your right hand and stand out from the side. When you feel secure, release your hold on the horn. Stand out straight, turn your body upwards, and extend your arms over your head. If you wish to appear casual about the whole thing you can fold your arms across your chest, eat an apple, or spin a rope.

To return to the saddle, reach forward and catch the saddle horn to pull yourself back to the horse. Take your foot out of the strap and sit down.

←—⟨⟨⟨⟨   **START**

71

## 28

## HIPPODROME, LIBERTY, OR COSSACK STAND

This is often used as a finish trick because the public, bless its naive heart, thinks the most difficult trick of all is to stand up. This is not true. For anyone with balance the simplest of all tricks is a stand in the saddle, especially with the feet in straps. You can learn this in a minute.

Place both feet in the Hippodrome strap which lies across the seat of the saddle. Some think it is easier to get into the trick on the run and some argue that you should put your feet in the holds before starting the horse. That is up to the individual. In either case keep a firm grip on the mane with the left hand and on the horn with the right until you are actually on your feet in the saddle.

With the horse running, stand up, releasing your hold on the horn. When you feel solid and secure, release the hold on the mane. Some riders find it helps to maintain their balance if they lean a little forward, but try to stand straight upright. What you do with your hands is up to you. You can wave them over your head, hold an American flag, flash a saber à la Russian, spin a rope, pop a whip, or put them in your pocket.

To come out of the trick, catch the mane and horn in either hand and sit down. Now pull your feet out from under the strap and relax in the normal riding position. Probably the most awkward and precarious moment in the trick is when you have come down from it and your knees are tucked under your chin. At this moment you have almost no support and can lose your balance. For this reason work fast and there won't be time to fall.

**Bernice Dean doing a Hippodrome Stand.**

## THE DRUNKEN RIDE

This ride is similar to the Hippodrome Stand but is much more reckless in both appearance and execution. Ty Stokes, famed Colored cowboy of a decade ago, was known to perform this feat so wildly that he occasionally threw his horse.

To convert a Hippodrome Stand to a Drunken Ride you need a whiskey or beer bottle. You do not need to drink the contents to be able to do the trick, however. Stand up on the horse and weave your body from side to side as you go down the track and wave the bottle around in the air. The more you lean over the harder it is for your horse to maintain a straight course. He, too, assumes the wobble and off-balance stagger as he weaves down the track.

This weaving of both horse and rider is what makes the Drunken Ride much more difficult and dangerous than the common Hippo-drome Stand.

Ty Stokes did not use a trained trick-riding horse very often when performing this pet trick of his. The green horses he usually bor-rowed could be depended upon to lose their balance easily, increasing the drunken appearance of both horse and rider.

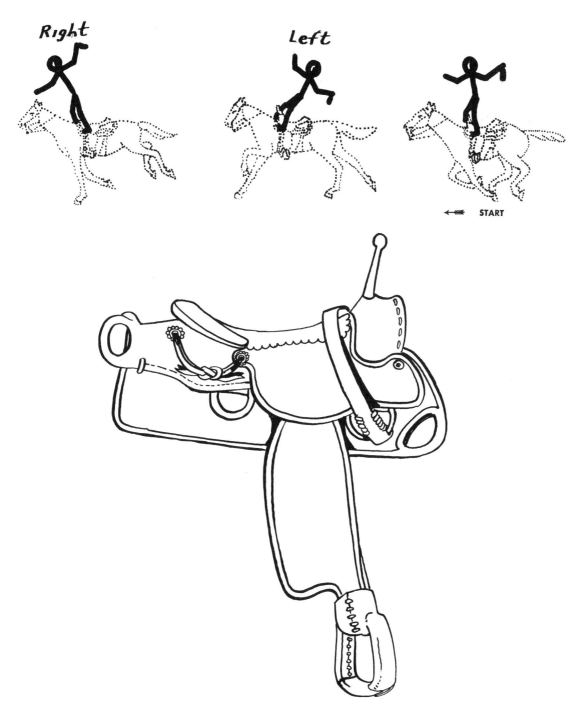

Right    Left

← START

The "Hippodrome Strap" is fastened to the rigging rings of the saddle

75

## THE BACKWARD HIPPODROME STAND

The mere fact that this is done facing backwards makes it quite different from the standard Hippodrome Stand. You will have to catch your balance by watching the horse's rump instead of its head, will lean a little backward instead of forward to hold the stand, and you will find that you are conscious of a sideways roll to the canter that did not bother you in the forward stand. You will find it is the hardest of all the strap stands.

Start the Backward Hippodrome Stand by sitting backward on the neck. Once again you may wait until the horse is going to put your feet in the holds or you can put them in while still standing still. Put your feet in the Hippodrome strap, grab the cantle of the saddle or take the saddle strings. Now stand up with your hands free. Better keep them readily available to catch something in case you lose your balance.

Do not attempt to get into the standing position until the horse is running as the lurch of the start will throw you forward toward the tail. When the horse is cantering, rise to your feet rapidly, check your balance for a moment, and then release your hands.

To get out of the trick, the rider comes down to a sitting position on the neck, holds the horn with the right hand and uses the left hand to help get his feet from the Hippodrome strap. The trick is completed by a Half Horn Spin to the saddle. If the run is short it is sometimes

**Bernice Dean doing a Backward Hippodrome Stand**

necessary to stay on the neck with the feet still in the holds and stop the horse by reaching behind to catch the reins. If possible, get your feet free of the holds, whether you have time to turn around or not.

It goes without saying that for all the Stands it is permissable to hold saddle strings or the mane for your balance until you are quite proficient. Free hand stands are not quite as easy as eating a fried egg. Hold onto something as long as you wish, but remember that the Hippodrome Stands are not complete until done with the hands free.

←⟶ START

77

# HIPPODROME STAND BACK OF THE CANTLE

**Juanita Gray doing a Hippodrome Stand in Back of the Cantle**

This trick is usually done in conjunction with a drag off the rump, as by itself it is too similar to the other stands to have much value. It must, however, be learned apart from the drag to be done with the greatest entertainment value.

Slide back to straddle the horse's rump and put your feet into a Hippodrome strap which is behind the cantle. This strap is fastened to the rear rigging-rings and is loose enough to slide b o t h feet into easily.

With both feet securely under the strap, grab the horn and lift yourself into a standing position. Put both hands high in the air, lean a little forward, watch the top of your horse's head to help keep your balance, and hold the stand to the end of the run.

To get out, sit down on the rump, catching hold of the horn as you go down. Take your feet out from under the strap and hoist yourself back into the saddle where you get control of the horse again to stop at the station.

The other method of presenting this trick is to hold the standing position for a moment and then fall over backwards into a back drag For further details see "Back Drag" No. 42.

## THE JACK WRIGHT DRAG

This is another trick named after its originator. It requires an extra strap hold known as a pick-up strap. Briefly this is a strap (see page 16) buckled through the saddle fork which is long enough for the rider to hold in his hand and drop low.

Take the pick-up strap in your left hand, but temporarily also hold the horn with your left hand. Keep your left foot in the stirrup. Swing your right leg over the cantle to a standing position on the side. Hold a saddle-string on the back of the saddle. This string should have a knot tied at the proper length to prevent the hand from slipping.

Now lower yourself, let go of the horn and hold only the pick-up strap and saddle-string. This will let you down an extra ten inches. Extend your right leg under the horse's belly and hang as low as possible. You should be very nearly scraping the ground with your back pants pocket.

To return to the saddle, hit the ground with the right leg to help propel you back into the saddle. Grab the horn with your right hand as soon as you can and swing into the saddle.

**Louie Cabral doing a Jack Wright Drag**

← START

## STIRRUP OVER THE HORN RIDE

This is a trick which can look very strange and leave the audience guessing about what exactly went on.

Turn to the left sitting sideways and reach down to bring the left stirrup up between your legs. Hook the stirrup over the horn across your right thigh. Cross your legs with a scissors hold on the stirrup leather. Lean forward and grasp a handful of mane to pull yourself ahead as you slide down into a sitting position straddling the stirrup leather.

There you are, strapped to the side of the horse! With utmost confidence you can now throw your arms into the air and ride free. It will look as though you are glued to the horse's shoulder by the back. The further you can lean forward the better the trick will look.

To return to the saddle reach back to get the horn with your right hand and the cantle of the saddle with your left. Now hoist yourself back into the saddle, unhook the stirrup from the horn and swing your right leg back over the neck to its own side.

Caution: Be sure the stirrup is well hooked and firm on the saddle horn. If the stirrup comes off you may have simply thrown yourself out into space. This will thrill the audience but is hardly worth it.

A variation of this is shown in the photograph of Jeanne Abbott, one of our best-known girl riders, who used this stunt when performing with a broken ankle to fulfill a rodeo contract.

**The Stirrup Over the Horn Ride done by Jeanne Abbott**

← START

81

# INDIAN SQUAT

**Louie Cabral doing an Indian Squat**

Some tricks are far more difficult than they appear and this is one of them. The first part requires balance and the second requires co-ordination, and neither part looks very hard. This is a good trick to practice at a standstill or even on the ground until you get a good feel for it.

Grasp the horn with both hands and throw your right leg up and over the horse's neck to lie over the right in a squatting position. When your balance seems good, release the horn and put your hands in the air. The trick can be left right here or you can carry on with the remainder of it.

From the squatting position reach back, twisting your body to the right and grab the cantle with both hands. Now raise yourself into the air by pushing with both your arms and legs. Throw yourself toward the horse's head and you will go over the horn, turn in the air because of your crossed legs, and come down astride the neck facing backwards! From here you can either horn spin or vault back into the saddle.

This trick is not child's play. Perfect your form before doing it on a running horse since unless you have good form or a cast-iron right leg you will remove bits of skin from your shin.

← START

83

## HOOKER ARM DRAG

George Hooker of the 101 Ranch Wild West Show, a few years after the turn of the century, originated a trick which has since been used by every clown trick rider and a few straight riders as well. The trick makes the rider appear to be walking beside his running horse and does look rather strange.

Throw your right leg over the horn to the left side and stand in the left stirrup. Take the left front saddle-string in your right hand as shown in the drawing, then hook your elbow over the horn. Free your left foot from the stirrup.

You can now slide down the side of the horse keeping your feet off the ground by hanging from your elbow. You can do what you wish with your left hand. Now start taking very long, slow steps in the air and you will appear to be walking beside the horse. The illusion is even better if you can touch the ground with your toes.

To get out of the trick, reach up and catch the horn with your left hand, release your hold on the saddle-string with the right, and let your arm slide around to catch the horn. With both hands secure you vault into the saddle.

**Smokey Chism doing the Hooker Arm Drag**

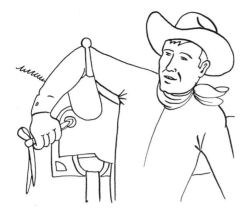

**Handhold for the Hooker Arm Drag**

## 36

## THE SADDLE SPIN

As a separate trick the Saddle Spin has very little value, but it is an important feature of foundation training, a connecting link between tricks, and between various parts of them.

The rider starts by throwing the right leg over the horn to ride sideways, holds the horn with the right hand while raising the left leg over the cantle to put him in a backward position. The horn is released and the rider turns his body to the left to reach the horn with the left hand, then crosses the right leg over the cantle to go to a sideways position on the right of the horse. The horn is released as the rider swings the left leg over the saddle to face forward again.

Some riders develop the knack of raising one leg before the other is all the way down and do a faster, better-looking spin whether in the saddle, on the rump, or around the horn. Don Wilcox, one of our star riders, does even these simple stunts with a speed and grace that amazes other riders. It just proves to what lengths Don will go to be "tops" in presenting any trick-riding stunt.

← START

# THE RUMP SPIN

The rider doing this spin goes through practically the same motions of those mentioned for the Saddle Spin. The main difference is the use of the crupper handholds instead of the saddlehorn as the rider turns from forward to backward on the rump of the horse. There are very few uses for the spin but it has a definite value as a training aid, for the trick rider should be master of any position he assumes, intentionally or accidentally, while on his horse.

←≪≪  START

**The Rump Spin being shown by Dick Borello**

**Smokey Chism doing Saddle Scissors**

## SCISSORS IN THE SADDLE

Although the horn spin and saddle spin will serve to get into position, they are slow. A more efficient method is to use a scissors action which will throw you immediately either backward or forwards.

Simplest of the scissors is done in the saddle. Scissors done to a backward position is a snap. Scissors to a forward position is only difficult because you must swing high enough to avoid hitting the horn. A scissors on the neck is quite difficult and is considered a trick in itself.

Scissors to a backward is done by taking hold of the saddle fork with both hands. Have your feet free of the stirrups. Now stiffen your body, swing it forward and down, throwing your legs out behind you and crossing them in mid-air. Push hard with your arms, throwing yourself up, and twisting to land facing backward, legs astride the horse.

In crossing your legs, put the left leg under the right. When you twist in the air, turn to the right. If the trick is not done in perfect timing you will land slightly on the left side of the horse. Use your left leg and hands to push yourself into a straight position. Using the same handholds, the scissors can be reversed to bring you once more to the forward position.

Another saddle scissors is done by leaning over the rump with the hands gripping the crupper handholds at their widest point. Swing your legs high enough to clear the horn, cross them, and spin to land facing the opposite direction. This, also, can be done in either direction.

START

## SCISSORS ON THE NECK

This is a dilly. If you bruise easily you will always be a little black and blue on the right thigh from this trick. Your elbow may also take a gentle beating. But it is a nice trick.

Sit backward on the neck holding the horn with both hands, left hand on first with the right covering it. Now lean far forward and slightly off to your right, resting your right elbow and arm on the saddle. Working swiftly, you can swing your feet up, twist your body to the left to bring the left leg up high enough to cross over the horse's neck. At the same time bring the right leg up under the left and over the neck. Pulling and then pushing with your hands on the horn you can raise yourself forward again to a sitting position on the neck. This time you will be facing forward.

If it is desired, the scissors can be used from this forward position to return the rider to backward once more. The rider uses the same handholds and drops down as before to raise the legs for the return scissors. This is done with the legs crossing over the neck as before.

If all these steps are taken in one fast, smooth motion, the trick is not too hard. Unfortunately it is generally used in combination with others, since by itself it is not spectacular. No one but another trick rider or a contest judge will know how much trouble you have gone to in learning the trick.

**Ken Maynard doing Scissors on the Neck**

START

89

## SCISSORS ON THE RUMP OR HIP SCISSORS

After learning the preceding scissors, these should be a cinch. There is no horn in your way and your only possible obstacle you may never even encounter. It could be embarrassing, though, to find your legs wrapped up in your horse's tail should he decide to switch it playfully at the crucial moment.

To do the trick, the rider pushes himself over the cantle to get behind the crupper handholds. Gripping the crupper holds at their extreme outer edges, the rider quickly throws his body forward and down, hinging as it were on the arms, which push up, raising the legs so they can be crossed clear of the horse's rump. The left leg crosses beneath the right and the rider drops astride the horse facing backward. The handholds can be released at this point, if the rider wants to go into another trick. If not, the rider retains the handholds and does another scissors to bring him once more face forward on the horse.

Smokey Chism doing Scissors on the Rump

Smokey Chism doing Crupper Scissors

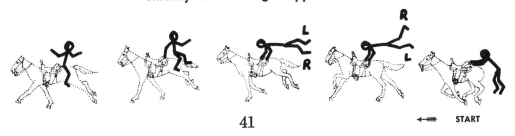

41

← START

## CRUPPER SCISSORS

It is recommended that you learn a straight Crupper before attempting this one. There is a certain "feel" connected with vaults off the rear and with it Cruppers are easy. Without it they will always be awkward and unpleasant. Learn the straight Crupper until it is as familar as a side vault. Then try this:

Slide back of the saddle, facing forward and place both hands in the crupper handholds, fingers down. Now jump off the rump and hit the ground. As you rise in the air turn to the right until you are facing backward, and land. You will now be astraddle the horse's rump, body twisted but facing backward, with your hands crossed, still holding the cruppers.

This is very difficult to practice on a standing horse. Fortunately it is not a hard trick if you are familiar with crupper vaults, so take a deep breath and do it on the run.

## BACK DRAG

Claire Thompson is believed to have been the originator of this stunt. As can be seen from the photograph, she stood up on the rump of the horse in what appeared to be a Hippodrome Stand and then suddenly fell over backwards to drag off the rump. Whether she invented it on purpose or hung up comfortably from a fall, she never would say. No matter how it was invented, it is one of the most spectacular of all tricks.

**Back Drag Straps are fastened to each side of the saddle**

Use two loops fastened to the saddle just behind the cantle. Usually the two rear saddlestrings on each side are tied together for this. A very loose Hippodrome strap across the cruppers can also be used. The loops are more comfortable and secure, however. Saddlestrings on a trick rider's saddle are much heavier than those on stock saddles.

Put your foot in the loops with the strap across the instep and stand up. Stand on the back of the horse as though doing a Hippodrome Stand. Now quickly sit and bend backward into a drag off the tail. Hands full length by your feet with your arms hanging over your head.

To come out of the trick rise up to come back up on the rump. Grab the crupper holds to prevent any tendency to fall to one side, and remove your feet from the loops.

Smokey Chism and Sunbeam doing double trick riding. Sunbeam doing a Back Drag and Smokey Chism going under the Neck

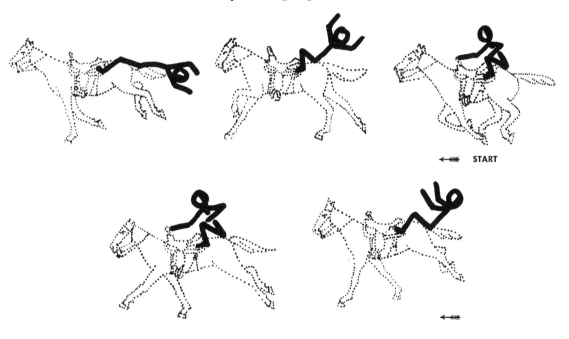

← START

←

93

**Harvey Rex doing his original Back Drag spinning two ropes, while Mildred does a Crouch Stand From the Withers**

## 43

## THE HARVEY REX BACK DRAG

Occasionally a trick rider develops who is in no way content with conventional accomplishments. That he is one of these unusual souls Harvey Rex regularly demonstrates during his trick riding, which sparkles with unorthodox features. His Back Drag is one of them.

The rider starts this trick while seated backward in the saddle and finishes it the same way. It is one of the exceptions to the usual rule of being seated naturally in the saddle at both the beginning and the end of the tricks. The rider seated backward, raises one leg at a time and puts the toe of each foot through the breast collar straps. Seated in this doubled up manner the rider starts his horse, pushes himself back of the cantle and lies down over the tail of the horse. The breast collar strap and the knee grip on the saddle both help in maintaining the rider's balance. While in this position he can add to the trick by doing something with his hands, and this problem Harvey Rex solved by spinning two ropes.

94

## 44

## MIDGE McLAIN'S BACK DRAG

In a way this, and the preceding trick, are technically not drags, since the riders depend on balance and not a drag strap. Be that as it may, the average audience in their naive way would classify all of them as tail drags! Here we will call it after its originator and try to forestall any argument.

The rider pushes over the cantle to ride behind the saddle, grips cross-tied rear saddle-strings or the crupper handhold with one hand and lies back over the horse. The legs are raised alongside the saddle to add to the illusion of the rider lying on top of the horse. You will note in the photograph that Midge added to the trick by spinning a baton in her right hand.

To get out of the trick the rider rises up to the sitting position back of the saddle, boosts over the cantle, and is once more seated in the saddle.

← START

**Midge McLain's Back Drag**

95

## FORWARD TAIL STAND

Tail Stands can be done well to look like a Stand, or they can be done poorly so that the rider looks as though he is biting the horse in the tail. Above all, rock into the Tail Stand determined to go down to the full length of your arms. Otherwise you will be riding along lying on your stomach over the horse's rump with your legs waving cutely in the air. The whole scene will be reminiscent of those baby-on-the-blanket pictures.

To do the trick properly turn backward in the saddle, or move up to the rump if it is more convenient. Take the crupperholds in both hands with your palms turned upward. Although it may appear to be impossible, throw your elbows out like a bird about to take flight.

Now, with a smile dive headfirst down over the horse's tail, throwing your legs high into the air. It will help if you bend your back a trifle to really get those legs up. Otherwise you will be pulled back down from the weight of your feet alone, regardless of the size of shoe you wear. Brace your shoulders against the buttocks of the horse and hold this stand the full length of the run.

To return to normal, swing your feet down to straddle the horse again. Give a lift with your arms to pull your head up where it belongs. You can now turn around back into the forward position or you can scissors back.

The best way to finish the Tail Stand is to cross your legs while you are still in the stand, then come down with considerable speed and scissors back into the forward position in the saddle. This can easily be practiced at the standstill and is by far the best way to finish the trick.

**Ken Williams doing a Tail Stand**

← START

## BACKWARD TAIL STAND

**Smokey Chism doing a Backward Tail Stand**

Ted Elder was probably America's greatest trick rider and certainly America's most ingenious one. He originated both the Forward and Backward Tail Stands. Of the two, the Backward is by far the more difficult.

Sitting slightly back of the saddle, but facing forward, reach behind you and take a firm grip on the crupper-holds with both hands. Force your elbows out as far as you can as this will give you aid in balance when you are down. Now lean backward and slide down via the tail, on your back as far as your arms will allow. Throw your feet up in the air until you are standing out from the horse. Hold this position for the complete run, snapping out of it at the end of the run just before the horse comes into the station.

It helps somewhat to keep your balance if you spread your legs, but with practice you will be able to do the stand with your feet together. To get out of the trick swing up and pull yourself back into the saddle.

← START

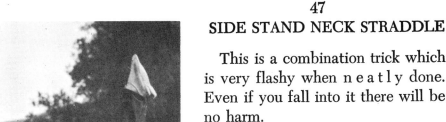

← START

## 47
## SIDE STAND NECK STRADDLE

**Smokey Chism doing a
Side Stand Neck Straddle**

This is a combination trick which is very flashy when n e a t l y done. Even if you fall into it there will be no harm.

Take the horn with both hands and then bring your left foot over the cantle to stand on the right side of the horse. Change your left hand to take the right crupper hold and swing forward with your head down by the left stirrup and your feet in the air. If you can feel the saddle touching only your shoulders you will know you are doing the Side Stand properly.

From this position let your feet wander off to your right to a little forward on the horn. Now come down with your legs straddling the neck, and your head up. There you are sitting backwards on the neck. Surprised?

To get out of this position you may use either a half horn-spin or vault off the neck and into the saddle.

The Side Stand can be used as the beginning of such t r i c k s as the Spread-eagle Cartwheel or a Saddle Somersault which are described later.

## SINGLE VAULTS

Despite the large number of tricks which can be done without touching the ground, a trick rider who does not know how to vault is no true trick rider.

The vault is the basis of all ground tricks and is certainly the most efficient way to end a great many. It is the vault that takes the posing out of trick riding and gives it action. It is the vault that is fun. From the vault you take wing.

Many trick riders advise learning to vault first, before starting anything else. It does, however, require a sort of irresponsible mental attitude to jump off a running horse, and so most beginners prefer to warm up to trick riding by learning top tricks. But as soon as your courage is built up, learn to vault. The first one is the most difficult, only because of the mental hazard involved.

To vault, start sitting straight in the saddle until the horse has hit his stride. Throw your right leg over the horn to the left side. Grasp the saddlehorn with the left hand first and the right hand covering it. Kick your left foot free of the stirrup and slide forward to the horse's shoulder, pulling your feet up into a tucked position. Now hit the ground and jump; as you rise turn to your right and lead with your right leg. You will fly through the air over the saddle and, as it passes beneath your right leg, pull yourself down to a sitting position.

When you hit the ground always face forward. You may not have to turn toward the horse if your jump is in perfect time with its lift. Otherwise you will have to turn toward the horse after you leave the ground. When you hit the ground your entire body should be facing straight forward and your feet should hit right beside the horse's front

**Art Moser doing a Single Vault or Pony Express Mount**

feet. The speed of the horse will put you in line with the saddle and your arms will act as rubber bands to snap you into it.

If you hit the ground facing toward the horse's side you won't be able to take advantage of the horse's aid in lifting you over. If you hit the ground back by the stirrup you will be thrown onto the horse's rump instead of into the saddle. There's a proper way and that's the one to use. Remember, the faster the horse runs, the more foward of his shoulder you hit, and so, hit the ground with the feet facing forward.

A vault done at the standstill is entirely different from one done at the run, and useless to practice in this way, so pay attention. You are going to learn this one on the run.

Have a firm hold on the horn. Hit the ground with feet together up by the horse's shoulder. Face forward with your entire body. Jump like a kangaroo. Turn. Pull yourself out of the air with your arms to straddle the saddle. That is the Single Vault.

← ≪ **START**

101

## VAULT TO REVERSE IN THE SADDLE

When it is necessary to be in a backward position in the saddle for a trick, a vault to reverse is very handy and looks well. It is not as easy as simply turning around, but if trick riders were looking for an easy life they would not be doing this stuff in the first place.

**A Vault to Reverse in the Saddle done by Smokey Chism**

Start this trick with the standard Single Vault but instead of coming up legs spread, leading with the right foot, you turn to your right as you sail through the air, leading with your *left* foot. Let your right leg just hang and you will land leaning slightly backwards with your left leg on the horse's right side, right leg on the left side. Turn loose from the horn and catch the cantle or cruppers to push yourself into position.

← START

You will very likely land to the left on the saddle at first. Use your left leg and hands on the cantle to pull yourself right. With practice you will learn to land a little more squarely. Part of the timing of the trick is to learn when to release your hold on the horn—as it is the holding of the horn when you are in the saddle that pushes you off to the horse's left.

This trick can be practiced for "feel" at a stand-still. While stand-you will have to vault while facing to the rear, but don't forget that when the horse is running you will hit the ground facing forward and turn in the air to face the rear.

This vault to reverse is often done in the same manner but to the rump or back of the saddle.

## 50

### DOUBLE VAULTS OR OVERS

Double Vaults often occur accidentally when the beginner is attempting a single vault. With perfect timing and a good lift, the rider may soar completely over the horse to land in a state of astonishment on the other side. This is not the time to let go and try to figure out what happened. Hit the ground again and this time try to light somewhere on the horse's back.

Don't be clumsy about Double Vaults. They are easily done when you concentrate on form. Form alone will carry you, so watch what you are doing. If your form is slovenly you will not only appear awkward but you will bruise your hips, which, if not unsightly, is at least uncomfortable.

Go into Double Vaults in exactly the same manner as you started the Single Vault—but this time keep your feet tightly together and use your arm to help shoot you over the horse. As you go over and come down on the right side, swing forward to hit the ground up by the horse's shoulders, jump again, and with the feet still together you will again clear the horse and be back on the left side once more. Double Vaults mean that you jump off the horse on one side, vault all the way over his back without stopping, hit the ground on the other side, and go all the way over again, back and forth for the complete run.

Try always to hit the ground as the horse's left foreleg strikes, so that you will rise into the air as his body swings up for the next step. This will give you the necessary "lift" to send you all the way over his back to the other side. Clean Double Vaults are almost impossible on a standing horse; but with the horse running they are quite easy as both the speed and lifting motion are used to your advantage.

At first it will help to go into a tuck on the shoulders before each jump. This will insure your hitting ahead, and will give you a moment

←◄◄◄ **START**

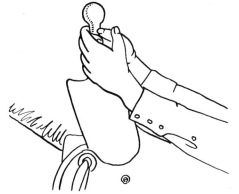

**How the horn is held
while doing Double Vaults**

to gather your legs together and get into rhythm with the horse again. With practice, however, you can do "overs" without a pause. Practice until you can do them "clean" whether you must always tuck or not.

Do not vault up into the air, bounce on your hip on the saddle and then go down the other side. It does not look well this way. It does not feel too well, either.

To stop this mad leaping from side to side, merely spread your legs apart and land in the saddle. It is wise to make your landing a few moments before reaching the station as otherwise the horse will have begun to slow down and will spoil your rhythm.

**Charles Ellet doing Double Vaults or Overs**

105

## VAULT TO A LAYOVER

For those who never manage to get enough lift to send them over the horse in a clean Double Vault, the Vault to Layover is a setup. It is a cinch. It was probably invented by someone who had so much difficulty he decided to make a trick of his struggles. Here is how it is done.

Vault from the left side of the horse as though you are to do a Double Vault. Hit the ground with your feet together, keep them together but twist to the right as you come up so you will land with your back across the saddle. Release your right hand from the horn and grab the right crupper-handhold.

There you are, lying on your back across the horse. Raise your feet into the air above the saddle and hold it. You can now lower the feet, free the right hand to grab the horn again and slide down the right side to do a similar Vault to a Layover from that side.

Usually in a run there is time for two such Layovers, one from each side. But the more the merrier, so practice getting in and out of the trick rapidly, and above all gracefully. You do not want to appear to be rolling about in a haphazard fashion with arms and legs flying in every direction. Do this trick fast, but under rather rigidly disciplined movements so it does not look like an accident.

## HIP VAULTS

**Smokey Chism doing Hip Vaults**

Sometimes these are called "Rump Jumps" or Crupper Vaults and both names describe the trick perfectly. They are done off the rump using the crupper-handholds.

Slide back of the saddle and take the cruppers for balance. Now swing your right leg over to the left side, releasing the handholds just long enough to get into position. From here you drop off to the ground hitting beside the horse's hind legs and in rhythm with him. Jump to cross over the rump and hit the ground in the same manner on the right side. Like Double Vaults, Rump Jumps are done from side to side for the entire length of the run. To get back on the horse, spread your feet apart and land straddling the rump as you started.

This type of Vault can be used in conjunction with several others and is frequently finished with a reverse crupper or reverse crupper roll up. Like Vaults in the Saddle, they are handy to know, forming the basis for other tricks.

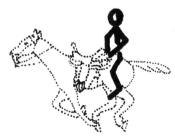

← START

107

## THE OUTSIDE VAULT

Here is a trick adopted directly from the rosin-back rider's routine. For this reason it will help immensely if you can learn it on a rosin-back horse before trying it on a fast-running small horse. If this is not convenient, and it probably will not be, work on your regular horse at a little slower speed than usual.

Go into a normal Vault, both hands on the horn, and tuck on the shoulder, hit the ground and vault very high, still facing ahead as usual. During the entire jump keep your feet together and draw them in as you go up into the air. Use your arms to push yourself even higher above the saddle and turn in mid-air to the *left* to land astride the horse facing backward. This turn to the left is just the reverse of the regular Vault done with a right turn.

Release your hold on the horn and catch the cantle—to keep in position. Now if you like you may go into another trick or you can turn to your left, put your left hand around the horn, roll on your left hip forward and off on the right side of the horse. Catch the horn as you come around to a forward position with your right hand, hit the ground and do a Single Vault into the saddle.

The entire secret of an Outside Vault is to rise very high above the saddle before attempting to turn around backwards. If you turn too soon you may quietly sit down far to the left of where the horse is running. If you turn too late you will go completely over the horse— which is another trick. The success of the Outside Vault depends upon a high vault with strong arms to support you in the air until you are turned around.

This trick cannot be learned on a standing horse. You will simply have to get the motions well in mind, start your horse and plunge in with complete abandon. There is little danger of your actually falling,

←◄◄ START

but it is quite probable that you will bark your shins on the cantle and may land in some definitely strange positions during the learning period.

This Outside Vault is so called only by the trick and fancy riders. To the rosin-back circus riders any Vault done on the ring-curb side or right of their horse is an "Outside" Vault. It is outside then, because all their stunts are started from *inside* the 38 foot circle followed by their cantering horses.

To these riders this is only a common Vault for it is done on the left side of the horse.

**Frank Dean doing an Outside Vault**

109

## ONE-HAND VAULT

This is not generally a trick by itself but is used as a finish Vault from some other stunt. It is safe to say that some of the men and most women trick riders are content to leave this trick alone, for few people have the strength necessary to carry the pull of a Vault with only one arm.

Actually the One-Hand Vault is exactly the same as the standard Single Vault, the only difference is that it is done with one hand. Most riders prefer to use the right hand on the horn when vaulting off the left side as they can use the elbow against the saddle-fork to get additional boost when returning to the saddle.

There is complete freedom of choice in the selection of the hand to use for the One Hand Vault, and so, if you find it easier to use the left hand than the right, do so with a clear conscience. The other hand should be flying in plain view above your head.

All of the Vaults are considered fairly safe since, if a rider's grip is lost, he may land catlike on his feet. Failing in this he will at least hit terra firma clear of his horse. That is the outcome usually considered, but the unexpected can, and does, add its hazard. In 1913 Otto Klein, trickriding in the Ringling Bros. Circus, was killed by a fall from a One-Hand Vault when he hit a steel guy rope stake at the edge of the hippodrome track.

**Smokey Chism doing Forward Vaults**

## FORWARD VAULTS

Forward Vaults are more difficult than Vaults Over the Saddle because the rider must overcome the backward pull created by the speed of the horse. For that reason you must go into Forward Vaults with a very firm decision to raise yourself feet first from the ground, almost as though you are about to do a back somersault.

Swing your right leg over the horn and to the left side of the horse, taking the horn with the left hand first and covering it with the right hand. Go into the tuck on the horse's shoulder and hit the ground. Face forward and *hit as far ahead as you can reach.* Now bring your feet up in front of you and swing them together over the horse's neck. You will land with your right hip on the horse's neck. Turn to the right as you jump down on the right side so that your left leg will be beside the horse and you will hit the ground facing forward.

Repeat the same procedure from the right side, this time landing with your left hip across the horse's neck, turn to the left so that your right leg will be against the horse's side and you will again hit the ground facing forward.

Forward Vaults like Overs should be done from side to side for the full length of the run. To stop them just do a normal Single Vault back into the saddle whenever you wish.

With practice you can make these vaults clean and hardly touch the horse at all. At first, however, it will help you to pause for a moment on the neck. Once you have the feel of the trick you can perfect it until it is fast and clean. Don't be reckless or haphazard in performing this, or you may kick the horse in the head, making him shy of the trick and thereby spoiling your rhythm.

Buff Jones, a top trick rider and roper of a decade ago, did these Forward Vaults in a manner that caused grudging admiration and envy among other performers.

START

## NECK SPLITS OR VAULTS TO THE NECK

This trick is a refinement of a Double Vault that bogged down and a Horn Spin. In other words, it was originally done by stopping a Double Vault in the saddle so that both legs were on the right side. From this position the rider pivoted on the horn to the neck. By speeding up this whole process the Neck Splits were finally developed making a smoother, neater trick.

Start the Neck Splits as you would an ordinary vault. As soon as you have hit the ground turn to the right so that you will be facing backward as your feet go up. Keep your feet going straight up in the air and over your head as though you were doing a back flip and sure enough you will land astride the neck facing backward.

While you are upside down in the turnover you can see your feet and aim them so that they will land on the proper sides of the horse's neck. You can also check them so they do not hit the horse in the head.

All the tricks which land you feet first on the horse's front quarters should be done with an air of consideration — since, after one good blow on the head, the best trick-riding horse will be tempted to duck the next time he sees your feet coming.

If you have difficulty with the stunt, it is a simple matter to go back to the way the trick was originally done. Start with a Double Vault and twist your right leg over and onto the neck as rapidly as you can. With practice you will gradually become able to somersault into the split.

← ◄◄◄ START

**Frank Dean doing Neck Splits while carrying a sword in his teeth**

56

## VAULT TO THE NECK WITH BOTH FEET ON ONE SIDE

This trick is a natural outgrowth of the Split to the Neck. Tired of the simplicity of landing astride, riders decided to land on the neck with both feet on one side. It was a nice idea and is a good-looking trick but requires practice, since at first you may land enough off balance to be unable to hold the position.

Vault off the left side as usual and hit the ground to turn to the right facing backward as you go up. Bring your feet over your head and keep them together. Now swing them slightly so that both feet will hang off the left side as you land sitting sideways on the neck.

Like the Split to the Neck, you actually perform a somersault in the air to land facing backward.

To get back to the saddle do a roll off the shoulder and vault.

←≪ **START**

113

## NECK SPLIT LANDING FORWARD ON THE NECK

If your ambition has been to tie yourself up in knots, here is the answer to your problem. Any trick rider will admit that the first time he did this one he was not sure whether he was coming or going. This is about as close as a trick rider ever comes to being a Whirling Dervish. Here is why.

Start with a normal Vault. Hit the ground facing forward, turn to the right as you come up so that you are facing backward. Your feet go up and over your head in a somersault. But cross them. When you hit the neck with your legs crossed and your weight comes down something has to happen. Your legs uncross by spinning you once around in the air somewhere above the crest of the horse's neck. Sure enough, you come to land straddling the neck and are facing forward again.

Some riders find that they can hold the horn all through this trick and some find they must turn loose to make a free turn in the air. Practice the trick at a standstill to get the feel of it and you will find how long you can hold the horn and still make the turn.

You can practice this first at a standstill, using a box so that you will be able to jump high and get an accurate impression of the feel for the trick.

## NECK SPLIT MISSING THE NECK

There is little question but that this trick is the natural outgrowth of an inability to do the Vault to the Neck with Both Feet on One Side.

Riders who cannot for the life of them land on the neck accurately enough to stay there are devoted to this variation. Many of the more difficult tricks are based upon the philosophy that if you are going to fall you might as well figure out how to convert it into a trick.

Whip into this just as though you intend to land sitting on the neck, facing sideways, with both feet dangling off to the horse's left side. But instead of sitting there and taking it easy, keep on going without a pause. Turn your body to the left as you come down. This will make you hit the ground again and you will be facing forward in proper vaulting position.

When you start learning the trick it is wise to aim for the neck and then slide down the horse's shoulder, making the turn against him. This will give you time to collect your legs and get set for a strong vault back into the saddle. Later you can refine it so that you make the turnover in the air and back to the ground hardly touching the horse with your body. Keep your feet tightly together and this will be a very good-looking trick.

## VAULT OVER THE NECK TO A SPIN TO THE SADDLE

This stunt was originated by Buff Brady, Jr., who holds a unique place in the annals of our great trick riders. As a champion following a champion, the "like father, like son" relationship in the Brady family is rare.

This creation of Buff's illustrates how each true champion manages, through his ability and training, to extend the trick-riding possibilities.

The trick itself is a continuation of No. 56, wherein the rider vaults to land sitting sideways on the neck of the horse. A bit of handhold detail is necessary now. Most riders prefer a 7-inch ball-top horn for all these vaulting tricks. The right palm is held on *top* of the ball as an upper pivot point while the left hand grips the horn below the ball. With this grip, when the rider's body is above the horn in a somersault, he is able to support his weight and pivot at the same time. In fact, this grip is of distinct advantage here; much better than the hold used for double vaults, since it is possible for the rider to rise higher above the horse by pushing down on the horn as he goes over it.

With this handhold the rider starts his vault alongside the horse, rises and twists as he goes over the horn to bring both feet to left side of the horse's neck; then, holding his body weight with the aid of the palm pivot, he swings out and to the rear to land facing forward astride the saddle.

This is all done in one continuous, smooth flow of movement with no stopover on the horse's neck for rest and revamping of plans! Don't laugh, you may do this very thing the first few times you try.

START

## COSSACK SADDLE SPLIT

The Cossacks have a small horn at both ends of their saddle. When doing vaults of any kind, one hand is held on the horn and the other holds a leather thong tied at the base of the horn. From the rear horn and thong the rider can do Splits to the Saddle in the same manner as the Neck Splits are done.

Although American trick riders do not use this double horn arrangement, they, too, can do Splits to the Saddle. The method is to use the crupperholds instead of a horn.

Start the trick by sitting back of the saddle. Cross your right leg over the saddle to the left side of the horse and grab the handholds. Now drop down on the left side facing forward and hit the ground as far ahead of the rear legs of the horse as you can reach. Vault as though doing a regular Neck Split and twist in the air the same way, but now you will land facing backward in the saddle. *Do not confuse this with a reverse crupper.* The Saddle Split is done almost entirely from the side of the horse.

Keep your right leg high or you will bark your shin on the horn. To some extent you can use your left arm as a brace on which to turn your body into the backward position. If you always take the crupperholds with a slight feeling of nausea this will be a hard trick for you. If you like working off the crupper handholds this should be a cinch.

**Dick Griffith doing a Shoulder Stand**

← START

119

## 61

### SHOULDER STAND

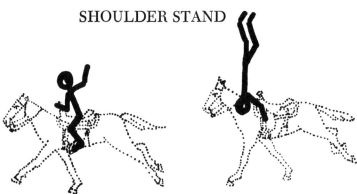

There are a number of ways in which a Shoulder Stand can be done, and each rider finds it necessary to work out some small variation. Basically they are all the same, however, and so only two methods will be described here. A rough idea of the trick is this: The rider holds the saddle with both hands, places the top of one shoulder on the withers or neck of the horse, and raises his feet into the air. The trick looks much like the headstand which small boys use to entertain small girls.

Sitting normally in the saddle, grasp the horn with the left hand, thumb downward. Put the right thumb in the shoulder stand handhold on the right side of your saddle. Lean forward putting your left shoulder on the horse's neck. With this three-way brace you can now lift your feet out of the stirrups, up to the saddle, throw all your weight onto your shoulder, and push your feet up into the air. Some **riders** prefer to raise just one foot to the saddle and push up from there.

Lean a little toward the horse's ears to help maintain your balance. At first it will also help if your feet are apart, but bring them together as soon as you feel able. Many riders find it helps them keep their feet together if they cross them as soon as they are up.

To get out of the Shoulder Stand there is the little matter of the horn to be avoided. Uncross your feet, spread them apart, and bring them down, pushing up with your hands at the same time. By pushing your head and shoulders up in this way you will not drive the horn into your chest.

Another variation of Shoulder Stand handholds is using both saddle skirts just back of the forward rigging ring, or the two latigo or cinch-straps for grips Some riders put small blocks of wood between the straps to provide an opening for their hands. With *both* hands on these handholds you put your shoulder on the horse's neck with your head to either the right or left, and push into the stand the same as before.

← START

Most riders use this method and seem to prefer having the head to the left.

This way you will have to experiment to find just how far back you should hold to get the best brace. In doing the stand your body should be nearly straight upright and your arms will also be almost straight to maintain that position. The length of your arms, therefore, determines the best place to hold.

The Shoulder Stand can be practiced on a standing horse to good effect; but it must be remembered that a horse runs with his head held lower than when he is standing. Therefore wait until you have done the stand on the run before making your holds permanent.

**Smokey Chism doing a Shoulder Stand, bareback, no straps, holding on to the hair and hide only**

121

## CANTLEBOARD SHOULDER STAND

If you are sensitive or bony in the shoulders you may not care for this trick. This is one stunt where it pays to be a little chubby.

Start sitting normally in the saddle. Take the horn in your right hand and step to stand in your right stirrup Now turn your right hand thumb down on the horn and grasp your right rear cinch-billet with your left hand. Put your head over to the left side of your saddle, shoulder resting against the cantle. From here you raise your feet into the air in a forward-facing stand and hold it.

To get out of the trick, bring your feet down to straddle the horse — but remember to release your right hand first. Use it to push against the rear of the saddle when you release your left hand to rise to a sitting position. You will naturally be facing backward at this time and so will either scissors back to forward or, in *coming down*, you can cross your legs and scissors to forward. This last method is very effective.

Frank Dean doing a Cantle Board Shoulder Stand

## SHOULDER STAND IN THE SADDLE

This trick is also a little hard on the collar bone. It is otherwise a fairly simple trick to understand and not bad to do.

Slide back of the saddle until you can grasp the back cinch-billets in front of your legs. Put your head down on the right side so that your cheek rests against the saddle fork and your left shoulder is on the saddle. Now push yourself up to your knees and from there go on up until your legs are straight in the air. Hold the stand for the full length of the run. Then drop back astraddle the rump.

The only hazard encountered in this trick is a tendency to lean too far forward, and, losing your balance, fall on the horn. To avoid this you may have to use the saddle skirts as handholds instead of the billet-straps for these will place your hands farther back.

**Frank Dean doing a Shoulder Stand in the Saddle**

← ⁂ START

## BACKWARD SHOULDER STAND IN THE SADDLE

Unfortunately from an audience standpoint this trick does not look any better than a regular Shoulder Stand and it is considerably more difficult to do. The very fact that you are facing the horse's head makes it a bit harder to maintain your balance. But that is not the real problem. The problem is to get your feet up. They become incredibly heavy.

Get onto the neck anyway you wish as long as you are facing backward when you get there. Take the saddle horn in the left hand with the thumb down. Grasp the saddle skirt with the right hand. Now put your left shoulder on the saddle and bring your feet up into a stand in whatever manner you can.

It may help if you keep the right foot in the stirrup to give yourself a slight boost into the air. Or, if your horse has well defined shoulders, you can actually place one foot on them long enough to give you a lift. Most important, of course, is to use your left hand to hold your body well above the horn. With the action of the horse it is impossible to roll smoothly into this stand. You will have to make a quick lunge into the upside-down position.

Practice this at a standstill. Every individual must figure out his own timing, push, and swing. That horn business is no joke, so do not dash off half-cocked. Another method of getting into this stand is explained in No. 119.

**Saddle Somersault done by Ken Williams**

← ⬤⬤⬤ START

## 65

## SADDLE SOMERSAULT

Many tricks need to be dressed up at the finish as the mere process of climbing awkwardly out of a trick can ruin its original flash. The Arabesques, One-Foot Stands, and Sprinter's Stances can often be finished with a Saddle Somersault and be greatly improved because of it.

To learn the Saddle Somersault — and to get the feel for it — start by standing on the horse's side with your right foot in the right stirrup. Grasp the saddle horn, thumb down, in the right hand and a saddlestring or the left-hand crupper handhold with the left hand.

Now dive out from the saddle, face downward, feet in the air. When the horse is moving your feet will be carried back alongside the horse, so, from this position as you are facing the rear, lift yourself up and forward in order to land astride the horse's neck, facing the saddle.

Be sure to keep your legs spread when you hit astride the neck.

Be sure that you go into the trick with your thumb down on the horn. It is from the hand position that you derive sufficient control to pull yourself up and forward onto the neck.

In combination with a Sprinter's Stance, place your left foot in the seat of the saddle, rise up and dive off. This finish is very good from an audience standpoint and not difficult, once you have become proficient at the somersault from the side.

Another good variation of this is in combination with Side Stand Neck Straddle No. 47. Both are done from the same holds. The rider can rise out of the Saddle Somersault into No. 47 or go from No. 47 into the Somersault.

## FORWARD DIVE OFF THE HORN

All tricks related to the Cartwheels are very difficult but comparatively safe. This is one of them. A beginner may fall often but he always falls free. If possible, learn this group of tricks on a slow running horse since speed is of little assistance — the lift coming more from the rider's muscle than from the pace or the up-and-down motion of the horse. It is especially true of this trick, as the rider's return to the saddle is *against* the forward motion of the horse and not with it.

Start sitting in a normal position in the saddle and take the horn in both hands, thumbs down. Lean forward over the left side in front of the horn and dive forward headfirst, allowing your feet to follow you over into a tuck against the horse's shoulder. Hang from the horn facing forward. Do not turn your body, but, using the horse's shoulder for a brace, bring your feet up forward into the air over your head, pull with your arms, and turn over to a backward roll into the saddle.

**Scotty Black doing Forward Dive and Pull Up Over the Horn**

If you wish, you may drop from a tuck to hit the ground with your feet. This will provide a slight boost to help develop enough momentum to throw you back into the saddle.

The harder of the two variations, naturally, is the strong-arm lift-back without letting the feet touch the ground.

A strong push with your hands when you are over the horn will protect you from being jabbed with it, and, if you are in good physical condition, the strain of the muscle grind will not bother you.

Note that there are two versions of this trick. In one, the rider hits the ground and takes advantage of this added lift. In the other and definitely more difficult maneuver, the return to the saddle is accomplished by sheer strength. The choice of method will have to be determined by the individual. If you have the strength of an ox, a weight lifter or a wrestler, the muscle grind back to the saddle would be a sensational way of showing it.

In the past twenty-five years, only one trick rider, to my knowledge, ever seemed to enjoy this herculean effort, and although he wasn't an example of the muscle-bound type, Larry Lansburg did the trick with ease.

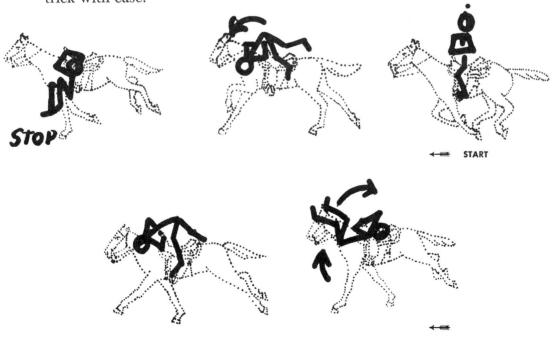

## PINWHEEL CARTWHEELS

These Cartwheels are based upon the Forward Dive Off The Horn, but are a complicated extension. They are beautiful if well done and incredibly jumbled if they are not. Form is, therefore all important when doing Cartwheels.

Begin in a normal position on the saddle and take the horn with both hands, thumbs down. Dive over the horn to the left, hit the ground, and turn out away from the horse to face the rear. Then push off from the ground, lift yourself straight so that you do not go into the saddle, and force your feet up into the air to the most perpendicular position possible. At this point you should be straight but upside down facing the horse. Let your feet fall forward, turn to face ahead and, as the feet hit the ground, turn and lift as before.

This trick is exactly what its name implies, a cartwheel, so try to make it look like one. You only hit the ground to give yourself enough lift to complete the circle overhead — and for that reason it spoils the trick to hold a tuck. Tuck when learning if you wish, and go over looking as if you have a case of stomach cramps, but do not enter exhibitions until you have learned to straighten out as you go over.

Cartwheels should be done for the full length of the run without any hesitation or break. At the end of the run it is a simple matter to twist the body slightly toward the neck when upside down; then spread the legs and come down in front of the horn to a backward position astride the neck. Or, you may rise from the ground, twist toward the rear, and land sitting forward behind the saddle.

START

**Chuck Chism doing Cartwheels with the bareback rigging**

**Scotty Black doing Pinwheel Cartwheels**

129

## SPREAD-EAGLE CARTWHEELS

For many riders these are easier than the Pinwheels. There is definitely more room here, too, for a rider's head.

The Spread-eagle Cartwheel gets its name from the fact that the rider has his arms apart. The right hand is thumb down on the saddle horn and the left hand is palm down on the left crupper handhold. Begin the trick by standing in the right stirrup, then take the handholds. Lower your head over the left of the saddle, kick free of the stirrup, raise the feet, turn to face the rear of the horse, and let the feet fall forward to the ground. Hit the ground twisting toward the rear and throw your feet up to a vertical position alongside the horse. Your face will now be towards the horse, but keep going until you roll forward past the horn. From here your feet will go toward the horse's head and down as you start around into another revolution.

There is no need for you to work fast in this trick. If it is neatly done with the legs rigid when upside down, and appears to be under control at all times, it is very impressive. Speed may throw it into a complete chaos of arms and legs which spoils its effectiveness.

To finish the trick, drop from the upside down position onto the neck of the horse or on the rump if you prefer.

**Louie Cabral doing Spread Eagle Cartwheels**

← ⫸ START

## 69

## CROSSOVER CARTWHEELS

The Pinwheel Cartwheels can be done uninterruptedly, first on one side then on the other, without the rider changing handholds.

If you are a perfectionist you will want to add this final gem to your Cartwheel routine.

To execute the Crossover a rider does two or more Horn Cartwheels on one side of the horse, then rises to the upside down position to fall over the horse to the other side and repeat them there.

All of the tricks having handgrips common to both sides of the horse — the Reverse Cruppers, Vaults and Neck Splits, Crupper Cartwheels, etc. — can be presented from both sides of the horse as "Crossovers," whenever it is unnecessary for a rider to change his holds.

← ⫸ START

## THE GRIFFITH CRUPPER CARTWHEEL

Dick Griffith, International Trick-Riding Champion, was the originator of Cartwheels Off the Cruppers. They have since been copied everywhere by riders who are good at rump tricks.

Start sitting behind the saddle with your hands in the crupper handholds. Jump off the rump to the ground with one foot on either side of the horse, hitting as far forward as possible. As you rise into the air in a high crupper jump let your head come down to the left of the horse, resting your right shoulder on the left side of the horse's rump. Keep your feet together as you somersault forward. Hit the ground with your stomach outward and then lift and twist to the left, and jump at the same time to get a "whip" and high lift from the horse. This whip will throw you back astride the rump.

It is best to go through the general motions of the trick at a standstill before attempting it on the run. There will not be any lift at the standstill so start from a kneeling position on the rump and somersault off to the left, twist when your feet touch the ground to be in position for the lift upwards. Try this a few times.

Then do it while walking your horse. With him moving you can let your feet drag till you are far enough back to enable you to crupper jump astride the horse. Then try it with someone leading the horse at a slow canter before attempting it alone.

**Dick Griffith doing his original Crupper Cartwheels**

←⇠ START

133

## CRUPPER JUMP-UP

Anyone who can jump at all can do a straight Crupper Jump-Up. It is possibly even more simple than the Single Vault. It is excellent when done in rhythm by a troop of riders and therefore makes a good trick for Trick-Riding clubs. It is also a good stunt to do over jumps.

Sit back of the saddle, grasp the crupper handholds with both hands palms down, and slide off to the ground. Hit the ground reaching ahead with your legs widespread and jump back to the rump. Like Single Vaults this is often repeated over and over until the end of the run. To finish, pull yourself back into the saddle.

← START

**Rose LaMont doing Crupper Jump Ups**

**Buff Brady, Jr., doing High Cruppers**

72

## HIGH CRUPPERS

To do a High Cruppers Jump-Up, most riders hold the crupper handholds with the palms upward which gives them a strong elbow lift. Jump high, allowing your feet to rise perpendicularly into the air. Hold that position as long as it is comfortable and then come down onto the rump again. When these are done properly they are nearly handstands on the back of the horse. You will find it easier to hold this handstand at first when the horse starts "checking up" just before reaching the "station".

There is a slight chance that you may at some time go over forwards from the handstand. If this ever happens merely throw your body to the left and convert the trick into a Griffith Crupper Cartwheel.

← ⭠ START

135

## CRUPPER WALK

A good comedy trick is the Crupper Walk. Announcers often describe it as the way a cowboy comes home from a dance on Saturday night. It is seldom done by riders in "straight" costume and never by women. It is simple, necessitating only the ability to do a Low Crupper Jump.

Slide behind the saddle and take the crupper handholds in both hands. Slide off the rump almost to the ground, holding the legs widespread. Reach ahead with one foot and put it on the ground, then start taking long slow strides in a simulated walk, stepping with first one foot and then the other on either side of the horse. The longer the steps, the more comical the rider appears. At the end of the run keep the legs spread, hit the ground in a jump, and crupper back into the saddle.

A fast-running horse will add to the comedy value of the trick by contrasting the slow walk of the rider and will also make it easy to get the necessary lift to crupper back when the run is through.

In this book we have tried to list all the variations of the tricks we could possibly find out about. There are still new ideas to be developed and there will continue to be.

After doing this trick for over 30 years your author added another original bit of hilarity to this funny Crupper Walk in 1958. He did this stunt with one hand, waving his hat at the spectators with the other!

It is quite simple but very effective.

**Frank Dean doing a Crupper Walk**

A piece of quarter-inch rope about eight feet in length is necessary. This rope is doubled to form a loop for the right arm. With the loop up as high as it will go the doubled end is passed across the back, under the left arm through the left crupper handhold to the right. The right hand holds the free ends of the doubled rope *and* the right crupper handhold.

By adjusting the rope, the rider finds the correct length to hold him in place when he releases the left hand. This is a safe trick for the rider is tied on *only* while the right hand is holding the rope ends. No knots should be tied in the ends of this rope for it must be free to slip out of the handholds if an emergency arises.

To get back on the horse, the rider's free hand is returned to the crupper handhold for a Crupper Jump back to the horse.

← ⫷ START

## CRUPPER JUMP TO THE SADDLE

This is generally used as a finish to crupper tricks to bring the rider back into the saddle.

Go from a crupper high into the air, getting as much lift as possible, and then pull yourself forward to land seated and facing forward in the saddle. Release the handholds just before dropping down in the seat of the saddle. This turning loose of the handholds can be compared to the "Leap Frog" jumps youngsters make over each other.

←⊷ START

75

## STRAIGHT CRUPPER TO REVERSE IN THE SADDLE

To do a Straight Crupper from the rear of the horse and land backwards in the saddle is a trick that is quite deceiving. The reason for this is that the twisting lift is obtained from only one foot! This resembles the lift from the side the rider would get when doing Reverse Cruppers.

The rider jumps off the rear of his horse as if to do a Crupper Jump-Up, but jumps back from his *left* foot, twists his body to the right in the air to land backward in the saddle. To onlookers it seems as if the rider gets his lift equally from each of his widespread legs. You may think so to until you try the trick!

←⊷ START

## THE CRUPPER DRAG

This is almost too easy to be considered another crupper trick but does have enough novelty appeal to warrant listing. It looks well when done on a dusty track, on a fast horse. The rider jumps off in position to do a crupper but sticks his feet into the dust and drags from this position. Of course he finishes the trick by doing a Crupper Jump back to his horse.

**Walt Heacock doing a Crupper Drag**

## CRUPPER JUMP TO A STAND

←◄◄◄ START

The lift for this trick is obtained as in a regular Crupper Jump. While the rider is in the air he tucks in his knees and bends at the waist to allow his feet to land on the horse's back. From this position he straightens up to a stand. A saddlestring from the fork, or a rope from the horn, or the rein-end is held by the rider as he goes down into the crupper. When he comes up and releases his crupper handhold, he maintains the hold on the rein or strap and uses it to balance with while he is in the stand. To come out of this trick the rider can either drop down to the back of the horse or walk up to a stand in the saddle. This can also be done without holding a strap or the reins. The rider then does a "free" stand from the crupper.

Some trick riders, when learning this Crupper Jump, land on their knees on the horse at first and gradually develop their lift until they land directly on their feet.

**Smokey Chism going into a Crupper to a Stand**

140

# CRUPPER JUMP TO A SHOULDER STAND

**Smokey Chism finishing the Crupper to a Shoulder Stand**

The rider does a High Crupper, and when he is at peak height, lets himself go forward to land on his shoulders in the saddle. His shoulder is up against the fork and his head is off to the left in an ideal position to go into a Crupper Cartwheel. The rider holds this Shoulder-stand for just a short time and either drops back astride his horse or falls over into the Crupper Cartwheel.

← START

141

## CRUPPER JUMP TO A HEADSTAND

This Crupper to a Headstand is done just as in the preceding trick except that the rider lands on his head in the saddle. The saddle usually has a soft round spot made into it to provide a head rest, This is up against the fork between the bars and runs into the gullet. It is about five inches in diameter and is padded to form a support resembling the so-called "doughnut" worn by circus head balancers. This depression in the saddle seat lets the rider's head become partly supported against the fork. The rider may only hold this trick for a few strides of his horse. He then drops out of it to land seated behind the saddle. If he misses the trick, he tucks in his feet so that he falls off to the left of his horse into a Crupper Cartwheel.

The handholds on this Crupper to a Headstand are the same as for a Crupper to a Shoulderstand, the High Crupper or Crupper Cartwheel. This trick and the preceding one were originated by Dick Griffith.

**George Pitman finishing his Crupper to a Headstand in the Saddle**

START

80

## CRUPPER JUMP TO A BACKWARD TAILSTAND

This is another of Ted Elder's Masterpieces. To do it the rider does a Crupper, tucks in the air as he would going into a Stand; but, instead of landing on his feet, he throws them up ahead, between his arms, and then rolls backward into a Tailstand. The hardest part of this is to make it a smooth accomplishment.

START

81

## HIGH CRUPPER TO A SPREAD-EAGLE CARTWHEEL

The rider does a High Crupper, and when he is at peak height, turns loose the right handhold and grasps the saddle horn with it. He falls forward, to the left, into a Spread-eagle Cartwheel No. 68 off to the side of his horse. To accomplish this bizarre gem the rider must be almost doing a one-hand handstand momentarily as he changes handholds. Dave Nemo, formerly a featured trick rider on the Ringling Bros. Circus, is credited with originating this difficult stunt.

START

143

**82**

## CRUPPER LEG OVER

This is similar to a Crupper to the Saddle, except that *both* of the rider's feet go off to the left of the horse and the rider vaults back into the saddle. The start is exactly the same as the Crupper to the Saddle. When the rider's legs are brought forward on each side of his arms, he turns his body slightly towards the left just before turning loose the handholds. This turn allows him to drop both feet to the ground to the left of the horse. The rider grabs the saddle horn for the vault back astride the horse. A more consistent way of doing this trick is to land in a sideways position in the saddle before dropping off into the vault —and this method is definitely recommended as the first to learn.

←◄◄◄ **START**

**83**

## CRUPPER ROLL UP TO THE SADDLE

Here is another of the numerous feats claimed to have been originated by Ted Elder. The rider does a Crupper Jump, and, when up over the horse, tucks his head to the left of his arms and rolls forward into the saddle. This is a great deal similar to the Crupper Cartwheel. The rider turns over *on top* of the horse to land astride the saddle facing forward! The crupper handholds are released when the rider hits in the saddle and he pulls himself upright by grasping the horn. If the rider turns over too far to the left he will miss the saddle and fall into the Crupper Cartwheel. This Roll Up can also be done from a kneeling position over the horse's rump — which is the way the rider starts when first trying the tuck. Later when the Crupper Roll Up is fully mastered it can be used as a finish trick to end a combination run.

**Smokey Chism finishing a Crupper Roll Up**

START

145

## CRUPPER SOMERSAULT TO THE SADDLE

←⇶ **START**

George Pitman added to the Crupper Roll Up and came up with a true Somersault to the Saddle. This is definitely a trick for riders of championship ability. Don't feel discouraged if you are unable to do this difficult stunt consistently. Few of our top riders can, although Cody Compton and George Pitman in this graceful accomplishment made it look easy!

The trick is started like the roll up from a Crupper Jump but the rider goes higher above his horse, tucks his head *between* his arms, doubles up to execute a complete forward somersault, *releases* the handholds and lands facing forward astride the saddle. This is a "free" somersault for the holds are turned loose while the rider is in the air. There is no chance of converting a miss into another trick — so, if you miss, just go catch your horse and try again.

**George Pitman doing a Crupper Somersault to the Saddle**

## REVERSE CRUPPER OR CRUPPER SPLIT

← START

This trick can be started sitting either backward in the saddle or sideways in the saddle, where it is possible for the rider to reach around and get the crupper handholds. Facing the rear he takes the left crupper handhold in the left hand and then crosses his right hand over to the right handhold. With his hands crossed the rider turns to the left as he jumps from the saddle to the ground. He lands on his feet, facing forward alongside the horse at a point a little to the rear of the handholds. The arms will be untwisted now, and if the holds were taken properly, both hands will be palm down. As the horse rises in his stride, the rider jumps in time with this lift, twists his body to the right, throws his feet into the air over the horse and pulls himself over into a backward position in the saddle. The arms will be crossed the wrong way, therefore to continue with another Reverse Crupper the hands must be reset to the starting position. While learning these Crupper Splits you may find it advisable to land on your left hip on top of the horse and throw the right leg up and over across the saddle as you roll forward into it. This will give you the fundamentals — but when you master the trick it will be done directly from the ground to the saddle without your body touching the horse.

**Walt Heacock doing Reverse Cruppers**

147

## CRUPPER SPLIT TO THE HORSE'S NECK

To land astride the neck of the horse from a Reverse Crupper, the rider hits the ground considerably closer to the tail than he does for the regular return to the saddle. He gets his lift, throws himself further over to the right side of the horse and pushes forward to get his right thigh over the saddle-horn. Before turning loose the crupperholds he pushes himself upright astride the neck. This method is considered preferable since, instead of coming down on the neck from straight over the saddlehorn, the rider's body is more to the right and comes astraddle the horse's neck from the side. Trick riders getting a high straight lift over the saddle when doing this trick have found that saddlehorns were not made to sit on!

**Smokey Chism doing a Reverse Crupper to the Neck**

## 87

### CRUPPER SPLIT TO A HIP ROLL

This is a trick that can be practiced along with your first Reverse Crupper. In No. 85, the beginner's method explained how the rider hit on his left hip on top of the horse. From this position now the rider keeps his legs together, rolls forward onto his *right* hip and then brings his left leg across so that he is astride the saddle and facing forward. In the regular Reverse Crupper, to land backwards, the *right* leg went across the saddle. By adding the hip roll the rider lands in a forward position in the saddle.

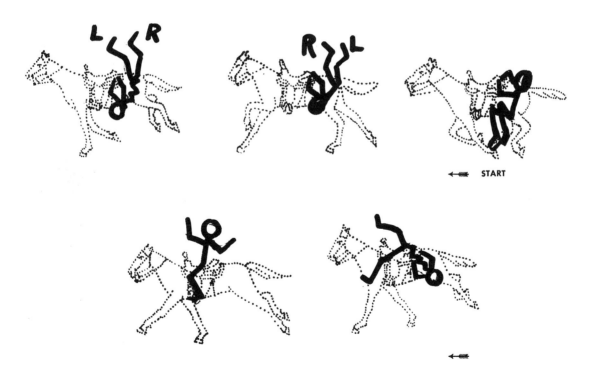

← START

← ←

# THE REVERSE CRUPPER FLOAT

To accomplish this the rider hits the ground and gets his lift in the same way as for a regular Reverse Crupper, but turns his body to the right and goes over the horse in a *stomach up* position to land facing forward, astride the saddle. Some riders find this easier to do when they jump to the ground further away from the saddle, towards the rear of the horse. This reduces the arc traveled by the rider's body and therefore reduces the effort needed to accomplish the trick.

**The Reverse Crupper Float done by Earl Strauss**

←≪ START

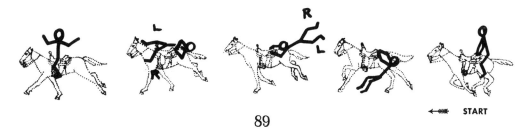

## CRUPPER SPLITS TO A STRAIGHT

This trick differs from the preceding one in that it is done with the *stomach down*, but with the legs crossed, as the rider goes into the saddle. This, then, is the same as No. 85, the ordinary Reverse Crupper, up to a certain point. When almost into the saddle, the rider crosses the right leg below the left, spreads them and drops astride the saddle to be facing forward from the waist down. Pushing upright, releasing the handholds and turning forward completes the trick. This is a "flying" combination of the Scissors No. 38 and the Reverse Crupper. If you miss the trick don't go flying off! Just keep the handholds if you fall and go into No. 51, the Hip Vaults, or another trick off the cruppers.

## REVERSE CRUPPERS TO SIDEWAYS IN THE SADDLE

This can be used to good advantage when it is desired to go from crupper tricks to horn tricks in the shortest time. There are a number of these — No. 81, No. 82, No. 86, No. 119, etc. — which are used in combination runs to tie the tricks together in a fast, smooth manner. This one is started in the same way as the Reverse Crupper Float, No. 88. The rider keeps his legs together and remains in the air a bit longer in order to land sitting sideways in the saddle. The crupper handholds are released, the rider straightens up, grabs the saddle horn and goes into another trick.

Combining various tricks for exhibition is well worth the time and effort of practice and it is certainly the unmistakeable gauge of a top rider's ability. One year Kermit Maynard did more than 50 different tricks in only twelve runs at a contest in the Salinas, California, Rodeo. His was an average of more than 4 tricks per run.

**Frank Dean doing a Reverse Crupper to Sideways in the Saddle**

← START

To increase variety, trick riders add other accomplishments to their riding ability
as demonstrated by Bernice Dean spinning two ropes

153

## THE FERRIS WHEEL

This is one of the few tricks requiring an extra prop besides the standard trick-riding saddle. An easily detachable horn, must be mounted behind the saddle. This horn should be in line with the regular horn but six inches back of the cantle and tipped to the rear at an angle of approximately 60 degrees. An iron rod is fastened to the bars of the saddle, beneath the crupper handholds, to contain this special horn. A twenty-five-inch piece of one-half-inch round steel bar is flattened four and a half inches at each end. Two five-sixteenths-of-an-inch holes for carriage bolts are drilled in each flattened part and the piece is then formed to fit the bars behind the saddle. A piece of wire stiff enough to hold the shape can be formed first and used as a guide. This is bent to a sort of V shape that curves around beneath the crupper holds to be out of the way of the hands. The point of the V must be left large enough to fit around a three-quarter-inch nut. The nut is tack-welded to the half-inch bar after it is mounted on the saddle. Check the shape with the saddle cinched tight on the horse, screw in the horn, and set it at the proper angle. The nut can be welded solid if no changes are necessary.

The horn is made of steel, has a ball-top and a knurled metal or fiber sleeve covering its one-inch-in-diameter body. The bottom end is threaded to fit the three-quarter-inch nut welded in the frame on the saddle. In use the sleeve turns around and reduces the possibility of the horn becoming unscrewed.

This is the way it was devised by Kermit Maynard who originated the "Ferris Wheel" and used it when he won the championship at the

Salinas Rodeo in 1930. Many trick riders have tried to duplicate Kermit's prize accomplishment but could not master the timing required for a fast sequence of these.

The single turn is performed from a continuation of the Reverse Crupper to Sideways in the Saddle, No. 90. The rider uses the horn instead of the crupper-holds, and instead of landing sideways in the saddle, continues past and twists his body to the left while still in the air — to land on his feet alongside the horse in the starting position. This is repeated a number of times, and when done in Kermit Maynard's masterful style, it is one of the most amazing stunts ever accomplished. The rider can finish the trick with any of the Reverse Crupper variations desired. The "Float" No. 88 is ideal.

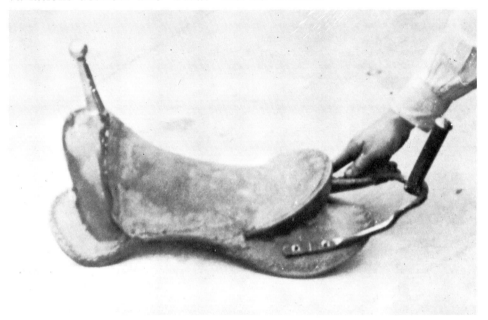

**The extra saddle horn used in the Ferris Wheel is attached to the tree in this way**

← START

155

## THE REVERSE CRUPPER ROLL UP

← START

Many of a trick rider's feats are easy to vary or enlarge upon. The skill and ingenuity of each rider appears in his own personal variations.

This Reverse Crupper Roll Up may have had its origin in this way. Just which trick it comes from is difficult to determine since there are many related to it.

It begins in the same way as a regular Reverse Crupper, however the rider does not turn toward the horse after getting his lift. Facing forward, he leaps upward, tucks in his head, doubles up and rolls forward off his right shoulder to land astride the saddle. The crupper handholds are released when the rider grasps the saddlehorn with his right hand to pull himself upright.

**The Reverse Crupper Roll Up done by Smokey Chism**

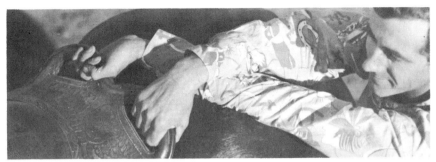

**The way the hands are held for a Reverse Crupper to a Tail Stand**

93

## REVERSE CRUPPER TO A TAILSTAND

A rider capable of doing both a Reverse Crupper and a Tailstand can easily add this spectacular bit of deception to his repertoire. At Livermore, California, one year Lee LeRoy asked Dick Griffith to show him how it was done. Both instructor and pupil deserve credit, since the following day and throughout the remaining performances Lee demonstrated his complete mastery of the trick.

It is, indeed, an ingenious combination of the two tricks the secret of which lies in the position of the rider's hands. The rider sits sideways back of the saddle, facing forward with both feet to the left of the horse, grasps the right crupper hold *palm upward* in his *left hand*, the *right* goes over the left arm to reach the left crupper with a *palm down* grip. With the hands in this position the rider jumps off, facing forward as for a Reverse Crupper, gets his lift, throws his feet above the horse, turns to the left and drops down into a Tailstand.

This whole sequence should be done as far toward the rear of the horse as possible — since it is easier and more smoothly executed if the rider hits the ground, twists, and goes almost straight up into the Tailstand. From the stand the rider can cross his legs as he lowers them and "Scissor" back to a normal position in the saddle.

START

157

## THE BILLY KEEN DRAG

In 1925 at the Madison Square Garden Rodeo a hitherto unknown stunt was done in the trick-riding contest and the judges promptly "goose-egged" the rider. They thought he had fallen off! This unexpected reception of his new feature made it necessary for the unhappy originator, top trick-rider Billy Keen, to change the judges' minds. To accomplish this, he had to repeat the trick again and again, before the doubting judges were finally convinced the drag was not an accident.

For this trick the rider sits backward in the saddle, takes hold of the cruppers with both hands, thumbs toward the center, raises his feet to the seat of the saddle and pushes over into a forward roll, with his head between his arms, off the rear of the horse. When his feet touch the ground the rider drags, directly over the horse's tail, until he is ready to return to the saddle. To do this he quickly doubles at the knees to hit the ground with his feet for the lift upward, pulls with his arms, and raises his legs over the horse to roll on his shoulders to a backward position in the saddle. To land in a forward position the legs are crossed in the air to "scissor" the rider around.

←◄◄◄ START

**Paul St. Croix doing a Billy Keen Drag**

## THE TED ELDER DRAG

Trick riders must often seem crazy. When they perform this out-landish stunt they appear to have literally lost their heads. In this Tail Drag of "Suicide Elder's" the rider's head is out of sight between the hind legs of the horse.

The rider starts into the trick when sitting backward in the saddle, takes the crupper holds, palms down as in the preceding drag, leans forward, pushes with his arms until he is far over the tail at arm's length — and then somersaults off to drag his feet on the ground. To re-turn to the saddle the rider raises his legs as in the preceding trick.

This drag is one that may require various deviations from the standard handholds. If the hands are too far ahead the strain on the neck will be severe. Setting the saddle a few inches further back may be all that is required. If not, perhaps you may want to follow Marco Borello's example and attach a second set of crupper-handholds to the saddle; or use a stiff cable sling fastened to the back rigging rings. Pauline Nesbitt, one of the champion Girl Trick Riders, used this sling type handhold with excellent results.

**Smokey Chism doing a Ted Elder Drag**

159

## THE ELDER TAIL DRAG LAYOUT

←◄◄◄ START

After a trick rider becomes proficient in his performance of the Ted Elder Tail Drag he may have enough strength left to accomplish this exacting addition.

The rider lowers his body as for the Elder Drag but *holds* the horizontal position, behind the horse, for a short time before dropping into the drag.

George Pitman ably illustrated to what lengths champions will go to outdo one another — when he added this "layout" to the Elder creation.

**The Elder Drag Layout done by George Pitman**

←◄◄◄ START

## THE SIDE DRAG

This drag, although quite similar to the famous ones of both Elder and Keen, is more difficult and definitely not as sensational in appearance. A few trick riders have mastered this. Outstanding among these was Glenn Porter. Glenn and the Van sisters — Tillie, Alice, and Florence — were all protegés of Doc Sahr, a great trick-riding enthusiast and a marvelous instructor. Under Doc's watchful eye all the problems that arose were carefully worked out. The value of this thorough training was well illustrated by the way Glenn did the Side Drag.

This drag is accomplished from the same handholds and is started like the Elder and Keen Tail Drags, from backward in the saddle. Instead of going off in a somersault *over* the horse's tail, the rider drops his head across his right arm, rolls off to the *side* of the horse and drags, face up, in this position. The difficult part of the trick is getting back up, since, as a rule, the rider's weight pulls the rear of the saddle off center. To raise himself, the rider quickly doubles his legs at the knees and kicks hard against the ground in order to get the upward lift necessary for the roll backward into the starting position in the saddle. This can be done from either side of the horse but here we have described the more common method of doing it from the left.

Occasionally in our listing of these tricks we have added more than one variation under the single heading. We are going to do that very thing again here. Dave Nemo, formerly on the Ringling Bros. Circus Wild West Show, and one of their top cowboy trick riders, was the man responsible for the following stunt.

When done in the Dave Nemo manner it is almost like a Crupper Cartwheel done backwards!

The rider does the side drag but instead of returning to the saddle, he misses it! Dropping back to his feet alongside the left of the horse the rider turns under his arms to spin back into the Side Drag position.

Naturally he can finish this by returning to saddle as we described before.

Dave Nemo could do both the Billy Keen Drag and this Side Drag. Sometimes he would come out of the Billy Keen Drag, miss the saddle and twist into the Side Drag as we described above.

That's another one for you to try!

**Smokey Chism doing a Tail Drag From the Side**

98

## THE SPREAD-EAGLE DRAG

Junior Eskew, an outstanding trick rider and a champion trick roper, made this comparatively simple drag into a sensation. On a horse that fairly "split the breeze" Eskew's performance of the Spread-eagle Drag was a thrilling picture long remembered by rodeo contestants. Of course he did many harder tricks but none had greater show value than this. Which simply proves that the truly difficult tricks are not always sensational in appearance.

To do this stunt the rider raises his right foot over the saddle and puts it in the left stirrup, holds the horn with his left hand, reaches back with the right for the right crupper handhold, turns loose the left hand and then steps down to the ground on his left foot — to hang in a spread-eagle position from the side of the horse. On a dry track the rider's left foot is the center of a spray of dust, reminiscent of the prow of a speedboat. To return to the saddle the rider reaches up to get the left crupper handhold with his free hand, kicks his foot out of the stirrup and does a crupper jump, or any other trick done from the rear of the horse, to get back in the saddle.

162

Frank Dean doing a Spread Eagle Drag

99

## GOING UNDER THE NECK

Going completely around the horse by passing down under the horse's neck was, and still is, one of the classics of the trick rider's art. "Montana" Jack Ray originated this renowned feat a few years before serving in World War I. He was only to perform the trick these few years, since Jack returned from France to die of his wounds in the Veterans' Hospital in Sheridan, Wyoming.

In a way this trick is a more dangerous accomplishment than its more spectacular rival, under the "belly," for the possibility of tripping the horse is much greater. The safest method so far devised will be described. A harness "hame" strap is looped through the fork, or gullet, of the saddle to form a hand-loop that hangs from the right side. This "pick-up" strap is the only extra aid needed when going under the neck. Before going into the trick most riders do a vault and split to the horse's neck, or a half horn-spin to a backward position on the horse's neck, in order to enable them to place the right foot in the left stirrup. When the distance from "station to station" confines the rider to a short run he *mounts* his horse at the station with his right foot in the left stirrup before starting his horse. Standing in the stirrup the rider starts the horse, maintains his balance with his right hand on the horn and squats down with his left armpit over the horse's neck to reach the right stirrup. The left leg is passed beneath the horse's neck to the left side and is held high enough to enable the rider to place the stirrup on the foot. The right leg is then passed under the neck, where the knee joint rests on the left toe that extends through the stirrup. This is important, since it keeps the leg from dangling and perhaps tripping the horse. Now that the rider is secure on both sides of the horse, he reaches under the neck with his left hand to grasp the "pick-up" strap from the right side, turns loose his right hand, pulls himself around to reach the horn with it and rises upright to stand in the stirrup. He sits sideways in the saddle, then releases the horn to raise the left leg over it and get astride the saddle.

A short-armed or small person may need a larger loop in the pick-up strap. Since it has a buckle it can be adjusted to a suitable length as experiment determines. A way to gain leg reach, when necessary, is to tie the left stirrup ahead to the breast collar.

**The author going under the neck of his horse**

← ◄◄◄ START

## 100

## GOING UNDER THE BELLY

In 1910, while on the *Young Buffalo and Texas Ranger Wild West Show*, "Montana" Jack Ray got the idea of going down one side of his horse, passing beneath, and coming up on the other side. It was just prior to the show's opening date in Peoria, Illinois, and the show lot was muddy and slick when Jack decided to try his new stunt.

Two other cowboys on the show, George Hooker and Ben Pitti, helped Jack rig his saddle for the initial trial. The three finally decided a broomstick, taped from stirrup to stirrup beneath the horse, would allow a rider to crawl across and come up on the other side. George and Ben taped the broomstick on and Ray was ready to go. George Hooker mounted his horse and led off at a gallop across the arena with Jack following him. Up to now everything looked as if it might work. But the boys hadn't tried out the rig while the horse was standing still, since all three felt confident in the successful accomplishment of the stunt. This small oversight proved their undoing. As Jack started across the broomstick, one end slipped out of the taped stirrup and Jack fell face up in the mud beneath his horse.

Falling in this manner gives a rider a fifty-per-cent chance of not being stepped on for he has only to worry about the two hind legs. But Jack's luck was bad and one mud-covered hind foot struck his head into the mire. Bruised, dirty and covered with mud, but not seriously hurt, Jack gave up for the time being. He thought of the trick again and again throughout the season; and then, finally, during the following winter, worked out the method used to this day.

The right stirrup is tied in place to the cinch or cinch ring with the foot opening parallel with the side of the horse. Usually a small strap is used for this, and it is fastened around the stirrup-leather just above the top of the stirrup. To prevent the stirrup from swinging, it is taped solidly to the stirrup-leathers. This will keep the stirrup in position at all times and make it much easier for the trick rider to reach with his foot.

Also, on the right hand side of the horse, two leather slings are hung from the saddle. These are to enable the rider to climb up into the saddle. The lowest sling should be in a position where the rider's arm can just reach it when he is hanging down from the other side. The upper sling must be high enough for the rider to reach the horn for his final handhold.

The only extra piece of equipment on the left of the saddle is the pick-up strap described in the previous trick.[1]

**Paul St. Croix of Red Bluff, California, going under the belly. Note the two slings and taped-up hobbled stirrup customarily used in the performance of this spectacular stunt**

---

1. Larry Lewis used an idea here that has a definite advantage. A half-inch wide strap forty-four inches long was fastened to the right stirrup, ran through a three-quarter inch ring fastened to the cinch and up to the saddle horn.

With this strap Larry was able to hold the stirrup up tight against the horse until his foot was in it. When the right hand holding the strap and the saddle-horn, was removed, the stirrup was free to swing forward allowing Larry more room beneath the horse.

---

←◄◄ START

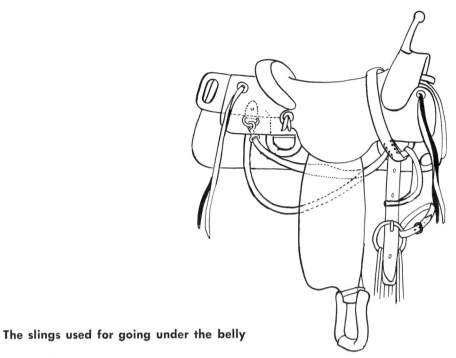

**The slings used for going under the belly**

When starting under the rider grasps the pickup strap in his left hand, holds the horn with his right, swings out of the saddle to stand in the left stirrup, crouches down and extends his right leg under the horse's barrel to put his foot into the hobbled stirrup.

He then turns loose his right hand and swings under the horse to catch the low sling, turns loose the pickup strap and pulls himself through to the right side to grasp the upper sling with his left hand. He is now in position to reach his final handhold, the saddlehorn, with his right hand and pull himself back into the saddle.

This method will be found ideal, with rare exceptions, since it has withstood the test of time.

Other trick riders have been known to use only one sling on the right-hand side instead of the two we have described.

Ken Maynard, motion picture and television star and formerly a trick-riding champion himself, recalls one contest where all the slings were removed and the contestants still were able to do the trick!

A knot tied in the flank cinch provided one handhold and the coils of the cowboy's rope hung over the horn provided the other.

You can see that a trick rider will do almost anything to win a contest.

## GOING BETWEEN THE HIND LEGS FROM BELOW

California's long-time trick-riding champion, Marco Borello, originated this version of going through and between the hind legs of his galloping horse. He is acknowledged to be the only man ever to do this trick successfully as part of his daily trick-riding routine. For two circus seasons he featured this stunt twice a day! His final trick-riding season was spent in 1938 on the Ringling Bros., Barnum and Bailey Circus where he was under contract to perform this one feature.

Borello's variation of the "Hind Leg Crawl" was different from all the other methods of passing beneath or around a horse, since he "hit the ground" in accomplishing it. That is, Marco started the trick in the same way he would ordinarily go beneath the belly of his horse. But, instead of reaching across for a sling on the opposite side, he reached for a handhold hanging below his horse's tail, pulled himself out, dropped his feet to the ground ("hit the ground") and did a crupper jump up to his horse's back.

The rigging used in accomplishing this trick was dreamed up, both literally and figuratively, during the contest at the Salinas Rodeo in 1928. Marco woke up one morning and said he had seen just how to make the attachments in a dream. He went right down to a harness shop and had the rigging made — and the odd part of it was, it fitted and worked perfectly.

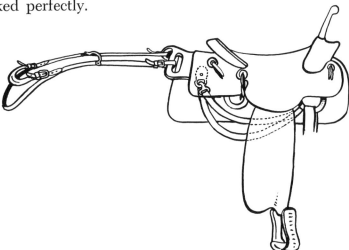

**The slings for going under the belly and the "Borello" rig for passing between the hind legs**

168

Marco Borello going through the legs of "Lassie," his famous bay trick-riding mare. This photo from the left side clearly shows how he had to twist sideways to go between the legs

This photo, taken from the right of a different horse, shows Borello's low handhold beneath the tail

He used a leather-strap, ladder-like affair that buckled to the handholds on the rear of his trick-riding saddle. This ended in a loop hung eight inches below a crupper that held the rig in place.

Marco's trick-riding mount was a bay mare named "Lassie" that "ran wide" behind, a perfect gait for this trick. Because of this many of the riders of that period claimed it was the only horse he'd ever be able to use. This was not the case, since we know of three different horses he used for this stunt.

This Hind Leg Crawl was little-known, regardless of the method used, and is still a rarely accomplished feat.

In 1938 the greatest circus bareback-riding family was the "Christianis" and they, too, were on the Ringling Show. Just prior to the Madison Square Garden opening of the circus, Marco and "Pappa" Christiani had quite a heated argument in their basement dressing room about the "Hind Leg Crawl." The Christianis came from a long line of circus bareback riders and believed that rosin-back riding was the last word in equestrianism. Justly so, no doubt, since nearly every conceivable stunt has been performed on the broad backs of these slow-cantering circus steeds. And, knowing the countless tricks of generations of bareback riders, "Pappa" Christiani was loath to believe there was anything new a cowboy could do.

169

← START

The outcome was that the entire Christiani troupe witnessed Marco Borello's first performance of his Hind Leg Crawl for the Madison Square Garden engagement. Then, and only then, were the Christianis convinced.

To accomplish the trick Marco started almost as if he were going under the belly, but used a rear handhold instead of a pickup strap to make it easier to reach the sling below the horse's tail. The two saddle strings on the left rear saddle jockeys were tied together to provide this handhold. He held the loop in his left hand, crouched down to get his right foot beneath the horse and into the right stirrup, then reached between the horse's hind legs to grasp the rigging with his right hand, released the left hand and pulled his head and shoulders out between the legs. He next grasped the higher handhold with his left hand, pulled himself upward to get the next handhold with his right, dropped his feet between the horse's legs and did a crupper jump to the back of his horse.

This is no trick to learn on a moment's notice. The horse must be trained to gallop smoothly, oblivious to the hindrance of movement as the rider's body bears against its thighs. To attain this uninterrupted rhythm the rider gets halfway through the trick while the horse is standing still, then starts the horse. He should be far enough out to be ready to drop his feet for the Crupper Jump. While the horse is led or ridden by an assistant, the rider holds this position, first while the horse is walking, then later at a slow canter, keeping it up until the horse becomes accustomed to the obstacle (you) or decides to get rid of it (you) permanently, once and for all!

## GOING BETWEEN THE HIND LEGS FROM ABOVE

A few years before Marco Borello figured out his version of going through the hind legs of a running horse, Louis Tindall — *the first one to ever accomplish it* — had wrested the World's Championship Trick Riding title from Ted Elder with this trick. The original method, invented by Tindall, was to go down from back of the horse, through the hind legs and come out and up to the saddle on the right side.

To do this stunt you will need the usual slings used for going under the belly of the horse, plus a piece of half-inch rope — which is to be tied at the rear of the saddle, run back between the hind legs and fastened in the center of the forward cinch — and a small stirrup that will slide along this rope. Naturally the stirrup must be put on the rope before both ends are tied. The rider sits back of the saddle, grasps the crupper handholds with his right hand, raises his left leg to the rear, and reaches back with his free hand to slide the stirrup over the left foot. The left foot pushes the stirrup backward along the rope and is joined by the rider's right foot which rests on the left toe extending out of the stirrup. The rider lets himself down at arms' length from the handholds, as his feet go forward between the horse's legs. He lowers his body as his feet go ahead and is finally able to travel far enough under to reach the right stirrup with his right foot and the under-the-belly slings with his hands. From here on the trick is similar to going under the belly of the horse.

This is a much more difficult feat than the Borello creation due in part to the use of the bare rope for handholds.

← START

171

## THE SLICK SADDLE STAND

← ⊪⊪⊪ **START**

This stand can be done either on the seat of the saddle or on the back jockeys. In either case the rider holds the reins, a strap fastened to the saddlehorn, or a long saddle string, in one hand, pushes against the fork to raise his feet into position and then stands upright aiding his balance with the reins or strap. The limited amount of support the rider can get from the reins makes the use of this aid the most skillful demonstration of the Slick Saddle Stand. Our phenomenal Dick Griffith accomplishes this stand *off the reins* in a nonchalant display of amazing balance even while negotiating the *turns* in a circular arena. When doing the Stand in the saddle the rider usually comes out of the trick by sliding his feet to the sides to drop astride the saddle. When done on the back jockeys the rider returns to the saddle by crouching low enough to reach the saddle horn with his free hand, then drops forward astride the saddle.

**Chuck Chism doing a Slick Stand bareback**

## SLICK STAND OVER THE HIPS

This stand is done back of the saddle on the rump of the horse. The same aid and the same start described in the preceding trick can be used. Or the rider can go into the Stand while seated behind the saddle. Quite often the riders combine this and No. 103 by walking forward out of this to the Stand in the saddle. To come down from the hip or rump Stand the rider can either drop astride his horse or crouch down to reach the horn and pull himself forward to finish astride the saddle.

← START

**Betsy King Ross, age 9, doing a Slick Stand on Back Jockeys**

## THE ONE-FOOT SLICK SADDLE STAND

← START

This trick can give you a headache in more ways than one. A slight swerve on the part of the horse is all that is necessary to provide it. It seems, for some obscure reason, that unbalanced riders nearly always land on their heads. A really rare exception to this happened to be unwittingly triggered by a newspaper cameraman. Marco Borello was doing the trick when the photographer startled the horse and Marco started head first towards the ground. Somehow he twisted in the air, getting his balancing strap between his legs, and hung vertically upside down with his head scant inches above the ground. The strap withstood the jerk of the one hundred and fifty-five pounds of falling rider and Marco rode in this unbelievable position to the "station". where his well-trained horse stopped to let the unhurt but amazed rider dismount.

**The One Foot Slick Saddle Stand as done by Frank Dean**

To execute a One-foot Slick Saddle Stand the rider holds the reins or strap in his left hand while doing a Slick Saddle Stand and raises his right leg into as near a horizontal position as possible. The left foot is over the center of the saddle at a forty-five-degree angle. Some riders stand almost sideways while others prefer facing straight ahead. Buff Brady, Jr., with his ballet training background, was able to do a knife split with the raised leg held vertically upright against his head in performing what was undoubtedly the most unusual One-foot Stand ever accomplished.

### 106
### ONE-FOOT SLICK STAND OVER THE HIPS

The Stands in the seat of the saddle are usually more difficult than ones done ahead of the forequarters or above the hindquarters. Between these points, on the gallop, the rider experiences the combined action of the two. Both behind and ahead of this area this motion diminishes. Stands done on the horse's rump, then, are only over the action of the hindquarters and are therefore easier. It's logical. But of course the only sure way you can tell is to try it yourself.

To do this One-foot Stand on the rump proceed as in No. 104, and when upright on both feet, raise one into the air. If the right hand is used on the reins or strap the right leg is raised. Most riders lean a little further ahead than when standing on both feet, and raise the leg toward the rear. There is no hard and fast rule and so, if you find it easier to raise your foot sideways, by all means do so. To return to the saddle, lower your foot and finish the trick in the same way as in No. 104 — or drop astride the rump and go into another trick.

# THE BACKWARD ONE-FOOT SLICK SADDLE STAND

**George Pitman doing a
One Foot Slick Stand Backwards**

This rare feature is credited to the originating genius of Montana's great trick rider, George "Pit" Pitman. To do the trick the rider rises to his feet from a backward seat in the saddle, holds the rear saddle-strings for balance and raises one foot into the air. This trick can also be done by turning from a regular Slick Saddle Stand to the backward position. When this method is used the rider holds the tied rear saddlestrings in his left hand, the strap from the horn in the right, rises to the Slick Saddle Stand, and, when secure, turns to face the rear. When balanced in this position the strap from the saddle horn is released and the rider lifts his foot to complete the Stand. To return to the saddle the rider lowers the lifted leg, then spreads both legs to slide down astride the saddle.

← START

176

## FREE STAND IN THE SADDLE

This is a great deal more difficult than No. 103, but it is started in the same manner. That is, the rider rises into the Slick Saddle Stand and then drops the reins or balancing strap to ride "free". To perform any of the difficult Stands it is absolutely necessary to have a perfectly trained horse — one that will go straight as a arrow to his destination. Anything less than perfection on this score may make an aviator out of what would have been a good trick rider. Try not to "take to the air" when you lose your balance, but reach for the horn or other handholds and vault back on. This may seem difficult at first but re-member all our top trick riders became adept at it, since they, too, often fell off.

← START

**The Free Stand in the Saddle is done on the seat or back jockeys as shown here by Smokey Chism**

177

## FREE STAND ON THE RUMP

This is the dyed-in-the-wool champion's rendition of the Slick Stand Over the Hips, No. 104. It is started the same way, but the rider drops his balancing aid when he assumes the standing position. These "free" Stands are the ultimate in balance feats and additional balance training will be a decided asset in accomplishing them. A simple device that could be used to build up this ability is the "Roly Poly" used by circus performers in a balancing act. This apparatus is simply a smooth round cylinder, log, or pipe from six to eight inches in diameter, approximately one foot long and a piece of one-by-ten-inch lumber thirty-six inches in length. The "rocker" or board is placed over the roller and the performer jumps on it with his legs spread to rock back and forth as he balances on the cylinder. To begin this *hold on to a solid* support and *step* up on the board to teeter it back and forth as you balance above it. In less than a week, if you try this for fifteen minutes a day, you will be able to get on and off and balance unaided on the Roly-Poly.

**Smokey Chism doing a Free Stand on The Rump**

## 110

### SIDEWAYS FREE STAND WITH ONE FOOT ON THE HORSE'S NECK

This Free Stand is done from a continuation of the Free Stand in the Saddle, No. 108. The rider places his right foot upon the horse's neck, and balances in a sideways position. Most of the rider's weight and balance is secured from the left foot. The right rests lightly on the horse's neck about midway between the withers and the head. A more difficult form of this Stand is demonstrated by the placing of the right foot between the horse's ears.

Smokey Chism doing a Sideways Free Stand, one foot in the saddle and one foot on the horse's neck

## 111

### CANTLE AND HORN FREE STAND

The origin of this trick is credited to Louis Tindall, who was a veritable wizard with the Free Stands. The start is from a Free Stand in the Saddle, No. 108. The rider places his left foot on top of the rolled cantle and then lifts the right and rests it on top of the saddlehorn. The balance and most of the rider's weight is maintained on the left foot as in the preceding trick.

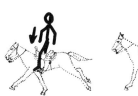

← START

## 112
## BACKWARD FREE STAND

The Backward Free Stand is done by placing the right foot on the seat of the saddle and rising into a Backward Slick Saddle Stand as described at the beginning of No. 107, the Backward One-foot Slick Saddle Stand. The rear saddle-strings are held for balance. When the rider feels secure these strings are dropped and he rides "free."

To return to the regular position in the saddle the rider spreads his legs and slides down. From this backward position it is then quite easy to finish by doing a Scissors or Saddle Spin.

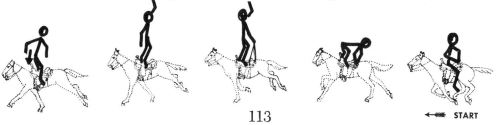

← START

## 113
## FREE STAND PIROUETTE

This is another of the cowboy conversions taken from rosin-back riding. The trick is started from a Free Stand on the Rump, No. 109. A quick jump and half-spin puts the rider facing backward. The rider leans toward the horse's head, to compensate for the speed of the gallop when doing the jump, and to assure his landing on the horse. If the rider just jumped into the air, with no regard for the forward motion, good old Mother Earth would be sure to catch him. The backward position is held a very short time, then the rider does another half-spin to return to his forward stand.

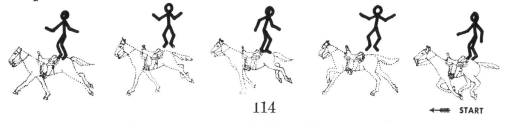

← START

## 114
## THE HEADSTAND IN THE SADDLE

Trick-riding saddles can be ordered with a built-in depression in the seat as an aid in the performance of this remarkable feat. This is a five-inch concave hole cut in the ground seat, and covered with the soft quilted outer leather. Generally this is located close to the fork.

←⚙ START

To do the trick the rider sits behind the saddle, grasps the cantle or crupper handholds in both hands, leans forward, rises to his knees, places his head in the built-in "doughnut" and then pushes himself up into a headstand.

If a good deal of pre-riding experience in head balancing is gained before attempting this trick, the neck muscles will be better able to stand the strain. A well-padded piece of wood cut in a triangular shape can be used as a support for the back of the riders' head. Paul Bond invented a support of this type which he used when he was *learning* the trick. An elastic band fastened to the wood formed a loop that, when stretched, could be slipped over the saddle horn to keep this head support in place. This triangular piece of wood is cut about five or six inches wide at the bottom and narrows as it extends up the height of the horn. The top is rounded to prevent any accidental jabbing of the rider if he overbalances. The rider drops backward to a seat on the rump when coming out of the headstand.

**George Pitman doing a Headstand in the Saddle**

181

## 115

### THE BACKWARD HEADSTAND IN THE SADDLE

When contest riders started doing Headstands they tried out every conceivable position. Some trials were successful and eventually led to new tricks, while others became just headaches in more ways than one. The Backward Headstand in the Saddle is done on the solid part of the seat near the cantle and not in a concave hole as in the preceding trick. On this account the rider uses a head pad held in place by an elastic chin strap. This pad is shaped like a large doughnut. To go into the trick the rider raises his left leg backwards across the saddle to stand in the stirrup on the right side of the horse, grasps the saddlehorn with his right hand (thumb downward), the edge of the right saddleskirt with his left, places his head as far back as possible in the seat of the saddle and then pushes up into the Headstand.

To come down, the rider turns loose with the right hand, places it near the cantle, drops his feet and at the same time pushes his head up out of the way as he lands astride the saddle.

← START

## 116

### THE HEADSTAND ON THE SADDLE HORN

After becoming proficient in the preceding trick the rider can proceed to a slightly harder Headstand. This one requires a few special pieces of apparatus. One is a cupped or scooped-out attachment fitted to the horn. Two famous riders developed different, although equally successful, headrests of this type. George Pitman used a large block of wood with a hole in the center. The hole was just large enough to go down over the horn in a snug fit. The top of the block was hollowed out to form a support for his head. The horn, when equipped with this attachment, looks quite a lot like the inverted "coffee pot" horn typical of Mexican saddles.

Ted Elder made his aid from metal. The small shallow bowl had a bolt welded to its underside that could be screwed into a hole drilled in the ball-top of the saddlehorn. Both of these horncups were easy to put on and take off. A helmet is a definite comfort when doing this Headstand.

The mechanics of this trick are the same as for the Headstand in the Saddle No. 114. Neck development as a prerequisite can be recommended here even more than in the other Headstands.

← START

**George Pitman doing a Headstand on the Saddle Horn**

183

# THE HEADSTAND ON THE SIDE JOCKEY

It is quite easy to confuse this Headstand with the Side Stand Neck Straddle, No. 47. Here, however, the rider is much higher on the horse and actually rests on his head. To minimize the possibility of the head slipping off the saddle, George Pitman added a thick rolled edge to the side jockey to provide the necessary support. This padded roll was included in the design of the soft quilted seat in the saddle.

To go into this Headstand the rider crosses the left foot over to the right side of the horse, grasps the right crupper handhold in the left hand, saddlehorn in the right, leans over (to get his head on the side jockey) and raises himself into the stand. The rider can come out of this trick by dropping his feet to straddle the neck exactly as in the Side Stand Neck Straddle.

**Billy Keen doing a Headstand on the Side Jockey**

## HEADSTAND ON THE RUMP

This is another example of Ted Elder's unusual creations. The doughnut-shaped headstand-pad attached to an elastic chin strap is worn on top of the rider's head. This pad is a standard piece of equipment with circus head-balancers. To do this stunt the rider gets backward in the saddle, grasps two secure handholds, raises both feet into the saddle, leans over to place his head on the croup or rump and pushes up to stand on his head. The distance from the rider's head to the handholds must be determined by experiment. If the saddle is equipped with one-piece crupper handholds that take the place of the back jockeys, the lower edge makes a good handhold for performing this headstand. The rear saddlestrings or the regular crupper handholds may be in a better position for some riders. This choice is strictly up to the individual. To return to the saddle the rider can drop back astride the saddle in a backward position or scissor his legs to land facing forward.

**Frank Dean doing a
Slick Stand spinning a rope**

## A ROLL TO THE NECK FROM A CRUPPER SCISSORS

"Smokey" Chism added his own refinements to the original Backward Roll from the Rump to the Neck of the Horse and came up with this unique combination.

←←← START

The rider hits the ground for a Crupper Jump, turns his body at the waist, while he is in the air, to land backward on the horse, (Crupper Scissors, No. 41); then he releases his right hand from the crupper handhold, and leans back to bring this hand over his shoulder to grasp the horn, thumb down. The left hand is quickly moved to the saddlehorn as the rider does a backward roll in order to land astride the horse's neck, "Smokey" Chism varies this sequence occasionally by stopping his backward roll long enough to straighten up into a Backward Shoulder Stand in the Saddle (No. 64) before dropping astride the neck of his horse.

**Smokey Chism doing a Back Roll to the Neck from a Crupper Scissors**

186

# BACKWARD ROLL TO A CRUPPER JUMP

**The Back Roll to a Crupper Jump done by Bernadette Cabral**

This Elder origination is well within the possibilities of the average trick rider. The rider starts from the normal position in the saddle, grasps the rear saddlestrings and brings them forward until he holds one in each hand at a point midway between his knee and belt. This is the approximate length needed for the successful performance of the trick. A knot is tied in each string at this distance, to prevent the rider's hand from slipping. The elbows are close at the side with the arms and hands held out sideways, almost horizontal, at waist-height. The rider removes his feet from the stirrups, lifts them to start a backward roll, goes over and pushes against the horse's rump with his hands to land behind his horse in position for a Crupper Jump. His hands, pushing against the horse during the rollover, straighten the rider out and prevent his landing to one side or the other of the horse. The Crupper Jump return to the back of the horse is done without changing the grip on the saddlestrings.

←⟸ START

187

## 121

### A STANDING BACK SOMERSAULT TO A CRUPPER JUMP

This is one murderous accomplishment that even champion trick riders avoid. They are content to let Ted Elder bask forever in the glory of the stunt that was responsible for his famous nickname, "Suicide."

He stood up on his horse, held a saddlestring in each hand and turned a complete back somersault, clear of his horse, to land on the ground in position for a Crupper Jump. The leather strings were strong and long to allow room for his turning in the air. This length interfered with the graceful accomplishment of the Crupper Jump and it was often only herculean strength that enabled him to return to his horse. Graceful or not, the mere accomplishment of this improbable feat has made the name of "Suicide" Elder a legendary one in the annals of trick and fancy riders.

← ◀◀◀ START

## 122

### THE "POSSUM BELLY" RIDE

This feat is of Cossack origin and was first seen at a May Day celebration in Russia, where it was performed as a double stunt. That is, two Cossacks rode the same horse; the one on top did a Hippodrome Stand and waved a sword while the other rider hung beneath the horse in the "Possum Belly" ride and played a concertina.

**The sling strap used for the
Possum Belly and Cradle Ride**

A long, strong strap, four feet in length, is necessary for the accomplishment of this trick. The end of the strap is put through the back rigging-ring, passed forward under the stirrup-leathers and fender to come out through the front rigging-ring and is then pulled through until the buckle is close to the back rigging-ring. The strap is buckled in place to form a large loop or sling to hold the rider. The rider gets into a *face down* position under the horse, with the loop a few inches below the waist, places one foot in the off-side stirrup and starts his horse. This stirrup aid should be omitted once the trick is mastered. It is a good plan to have someone ride or lead the horse until both of you have become familar with the stunt.

Always remember you must start and stop, or go from station to station in this trick, since you do not go into it or come out of it while the horse is in motion.

**Bernadette Cabral doing a Possum Belly Ride**

189

## THE CRADLE RIDE

The same looped strap used in the preceding trick is required in this one also. The rider gets into the sling *face upward* and adjusts the strap high enough to cause his legs to be held tightly under the horse. In this ride the performer can reach up and handle the reins but it is still a good idea, as in the Possum Belly Ride, to have someone else in control of the horse when starting the trick. When the horse is running nicely the rider can let go of the horn or tie-strings and bend backward to ride in a horizontal position. Both of these tricks, No. 123 and No. 124, are more suited to double trick riding, on account of the lack of horse-control by the single rider, and the not-to-be-forgotten danger of being tied and unable to fall free should a rider be "caught in a storm".

**Bernadette Cabral doing a Cradle Ride**

## THE STIRRUP SPIN

**The Stirrup Spin done by Smokey Chism**

During contest "Follow the Leader" runs this simple Stirrup Spin proved a Jonah to the inexperienced contestant. The rider spins completely around, off to the side of the horse with one foot in the stirrup. To do this the rider raises his right leg over the rear of the saddle, holds the cantle or tie-strings and swings the leg out, around, forward, and across the saddle. This puts the rider back in the regular position with the left foot still in the now turned-around stirrup.

Here the rider has to "bicycle". This is a term used to designate the unwinding of the twist of the stirrup leathers. The rider's left foot is raised as in the pedaling motion in bicycling. The stirrup unwinds from around the foot, when this is done, and the rider is ready to repeat the trick. The faster the stirrup is "bicycled" the better the trick looks.

Another variation of this Stirrup Spin is to "bicycle" the stirrup before doing a front-to-back turn. The rider sits straight in the saddle, "bicycles" his left stirrup, raises his right leg over the front of the saddle, spins out and around to land back in the starting position. When the spin is started the rider holds the cantle until he has to release it to let the left foot cross back over the saddle. These two "bicycling" methods are different and a few experiments are necessary to determine the correct spin the stirrup makes for each variation.

← START

## THE WALK OVER

This is a very simple beginner's trick that can be done easily in any kind of saddle. The rider raises his right leg forward over to the left side, passes it back between the left leg and the saddle and brings it back over the saddle to the starting position. The rider holds the horn and mane, if necessary, while passing the right leg beneath the left one. Ordinarily, the single handhold on the horn will provide the support needed.

← START

**Bernice Dean doing a Saddle Walk Over**

## THE STICK RIDE

**Frank Dean doing the Stick Ride**

A short, round, stick approximately a foot in length is used in performing this simple ride. A section of a rake, or broom handle, or a piece of a one-inch round dowel, will make this extra equipment.

The rider removes his right foot from the stirrup, reaches down to lift the stirrup over to the left side, inserts the stick in the stirrup, raises his right leg forward over the saddle to straddle the stirrup, free the left leg, and rides with both hands and feet free, as he balances on the side of the horse.

This ride is easier to do on a stock saddle for the swell fork and high cantle provide added support and prevent the rider from slipping sideways. If the stirrup leather length is correct this is a safe and simple feat to perform and is often used in comedy trick-riding routines.

## THE STICK RIDE BACK BEND

The same stick used in the preceding trick is also a necessary part of this stunt.

The rider shifts to ride with both feet on the left side of the horse, faces forward, puts his right foot in the left stirrup, leans over, raises the right stirrup across the saddle and places the stick in it. The left leg is lifted over the stick and stirrup, the rider straddles it, kicks the right foot loose and does a back bend. To come out of this the rider takes hold of the horn, rises up to get his right leg across the saddle, catches the stick if possible, drops the stirrup and is once more in the starting position.

← START

**Bernadette Cabral doing a Stick Ride Back Bend**

194

## KNEE DRAG FROM A STICK

This is started as in the previous trick, except that the rider places the stick behind his knees. The toes are pointed down and held against the horse's side for support and balance as the rider hangs down. To return to the saddle the rider straightens up, takes hold of the horn, releases his legs and straddles the saddle.

←⫘⫘ START

The Knee Drag From a Stick

195

## KNEE DRAG FROM THE HORN

This is one of the most tortuous riding positions imaginable. It is much too painful for general use and because of this trick riders are content to let Pauline Pickard be the only performer of this most unusual drag.

The rider hooks her right knee over the horn and places her left leg, at the knee, over the right instep, to lock her legs together as she goes over backwards to hang head downward. A long saddlehorn, preferably a seven-inch one, is necessary. To get back into the saddle the rider reaches up to grasp the horn and pulls herself upright in the saddle.

←≪≪ START

**The Knee Drag From the Horn**

**Bernadette Cabral doing a Back Bend**

130

## THE NANCY BRAGG BACK BEND

Although generally credited to Nancy Bragg, this trick was conceived many years before that charming rider won national acclaim with it.

The trick is done as a variation of, or in combination with, a Hippodrome Stand. The rider starts with his feet in the Hippodrome-strap and has the right crupper-handhold in his right hand. When the horse is running the rider rises, doubles tightly at the knees (to get as much room as possible they are forced ahead) and projects his stomach upward into the back bend. As the body is bent backward from this, the left hand is raised up and passes the rider's head to grasp the left crupper-handhold.

To come out of this the rider releases one handhold, then the other — and rises to a regular Hippodrome Stand.

197

## BLACK'S SPREAD EAGLE DRAG OFF THE NECK

**Drag Over the Neck by Scotty Black**

This is not a very commonly known stunt and as far as we know it was originated by Scotty Black, popular California trick rider.

To start the trick, the rider must be sitting astride the neck of the horse facing forward. We have already mentioned a lot of methods, both simple and complicated, of getting in this position. The rider might start almost the same way as described in No. 24, the Cossack Drag Over the Neck. Sitting in a normal position in the saddle the rider raises the right leg, to allow the right hand to go beneath it to grip the saddle horn and boosts himself over the horn to be astride the neck of the horse.

Now the rider is ready to go into the Drag. The right hand grip on the horn remains as the rider leans over to the left of the horse. The mane handhold is released as the rider's body continues downward with the neck grip of the right knee and the outstretched right arm holding the rider in the spread-eagle position. The left leg and left arm are free to dangle or wave. Don't worry when you try this stunt if your leg starts slipping off of the neck. Just reach up with the left hand to grasp the horn with both hands, let the slipping leg fall and drop both feet together to vault back to the saddle. That's how I was going to tell you to come out of it anyway.

← ◄◄ **START**

## THE PICK UP

This is one of the oldest displays of riding skill. Over 100 years ago here in California the *Correr al Gallo* was a common sight at the fiestas.

The Spanish vaqueros would race their steeds past buried chickens left with only their heads exposed.

With a grand swoop the riders leaned from their saddle to pluck the chickens from the ground.

These colorful, fun-loving early Californians had great pride in their well-trained horses and their skill in riding them.

Though not an ordinary trick-riding stunt at today's rodeo, we do occasionally see this skill demonstrated. I still recall that tall, agile rider Fred Weiderman picking up a neckerchief from the ground as a regular feature some years ago at the annual Hayward, California, Rodeo.

Picking up various things from the ground from your fast moving horse can develop your skill and add to your fun. Small paper bags with a little sand in them to hold them upright are ideal for practice. For competition put in a row of these, or handkerchiefs, and see who can pick up the most.

The Cossack Drag No. 23 can be an aid in accomplishing this pick up skill since *both* hands can be free to recover the objects.

Here, however, we want to describe the time-honored universal style of picking things off of the ground from the back of a running horse.

**Ken Maynard, trick rider and movie star, doing a Pick Up from a Cossack Drag Strap**

← START

To begin with, the horse must be taught to run straight and not swerve toward your displaced weight as you suddenly hang low at his side. This quick change throws the horse off balance and he must be prepared for it. If you have accomplished most of the other tricks in this book your horse will need no further schooling. If not, train the horse by reining him straight as you lean way over to the side. While you are preparing the horse, you will not be in position to pick up anything for you will be holding on with one hand and controlling the horse with the other.

When you feel confident that the training has progressed sufficiently, let the horse run free as you head him towards the left of the object you are after. Try to get him within 18 to 20 inches of the object as he runs by. You will be close enough then to hang low from the saddlehorn on the right side of the horse and pick up the article.

This is the general idea. If you want to reach down from the left side, do so, or if perhaps you cannot reach the ground from the horn handhold then use the "pick up" strap described in chapter 4.

This is just a strong strap with a buckle run through the forks to form an adjustable loop handhold. The size of this loop will determine how far the rider holding it can reach towards the ground. You will like learning this trick.

**Dick Borello picking up a hat**

200

## THE STEP OFF OR FOOT DRAG

**Buck Eddy doing a Foot Drag**

This is really a beginner's trick. If you can ride and your horse has been trained to keep going regardless of how crazily you act, this stunt can be accomplished the first time you try.

The rider takes hold of the saddlehorn with the right hand thumb up, covers it with a left handhold, and then brings the right leg up to the rear over the horse's back. This puts the rider in a standing position, left foot in left stirrup, on the left side of the horse. From here the rider squats to a sitting position on the left leg, releases the left hand, twists the body out to the right and lets the right leg drag the ground.

Some riders return to the saddle by reversing the action. A much more pleasing accomplishment is the one foot vaulting lift back to the saddle.

To do this the rider doubles up the right leg and kicks it to the ground for a lift back to the saddle.

When you do this over and over and gain confidence, you will find yourself going into it with gay abandon and be swinging off the side of your horse like a suit of long-handle drawers dragging the ground from a clothesline in a windstorm.

← ⋘ START

## THE BARBARA HUNTINGTON BALLERINA STAND

Take a beautiful girl in rodeo garb and a fast running horse, plus some trick-riding ability, and you have a sight to behold.

Barbara Huntington would fit such a description and her original creation combined a dancing school ballet split with her love of trick riding.

← START

The trick is accomplished with the aid of a strap that runs through the forks of the saddle and around the left thigh of the rider. The left stirrup is tied to the cinch and the rider stands in this to raise the right leg alongside the head in what is known as a ballet split.

This is a Ballerina Stand.

Many years ago at the Gonzaga Stadium Rodeo in Spokane I saw Buff Brady, Jr., do a ballet split while doing a One-Foot Slick Saddle Stand. The rest of us men trick riders, with no exceptions that I know of, have been unable to do this. Buff, however, had a background of acrobatics, ballet, and circus rosin-back training that made him an outstanding trick rider in every way.

**Barbara Huntington in her Ballerina Stand**

# THE SIDE SITTING ARM DRAG

**Earl Strauss doing the Side Sitting Arm Drag**

This is a quite unusual sight when done properly. I first saw Earl Strauss do this at the Cheyenne, Wyoming, Rodeo while I was trick-riding there in 1948.

The rider turns from the saddle to stand in the stirrup on the left side of the horse. The right leg is brought across beside the left leg. Holding the saddlehorn with the left hand, the rider reaches the right across the seat of the saddle and down to grasp the breast collar strap near the cinch ring.

With a secure hold on this strap the rider kicks loose the stirrup and lowers his body alongside the horse. When the left handhold is released the rider holds his legs out horizontally from the waist and turns out away from the horse to have his back against the saddle. The left arm is outstretched as the rider appears to be sitting on the side of his horse.

To get out of the trick, the left hand returns to the saddlehorn, the right goes over it to put the rider in position for a vault to the saddle.

←◀◀ START

## HANDSTAND TO A BILLY KEEN DRAG

**The Handstand to a Billy Keen Drag. Dick Borello on the author's horse**

If you are intent on suicide there are a number of trick-riding stunts that may satisfy you, especially if you want to leave this world in a spectacular manner.

A lot of them could give you this satisfaction if you tried them on a "green" horse. This one, however, might even give you a broken back when tried on a well-trained horse!

Dick Borello, son of Marco Borello the originator of the Borello method of going between the hind legs of a horse, did this stunt until his other rodeo activity, Brahma bull riding, awarded him a "trick" knee. So in his case it was a Brahma bull and not the trick riding that forced him to quit.

← START

Be that as it may, someone else will want to do this sensational trick, and so here is how it is done.

We will assume that you have already mastered the Billy Keen Drag No. 94 and are ready for this bizarre embellishment.

To start the trick the rider must be seated backward in the saddle gripping the crupper handholds exactly as for a regular Billy Keen Drag.

From here the rider goes into a Handstand over the crupper handholds. To do this he may have to raise one foot to the seat of the saddle to get the leverage necessary for the push up into the handstand. The handstand is held only momentarily at first and the rider doubles his arms to land on his shoulders for the roll back into the Billy Keen Drag.

Control the fall when dropping out of the Handstand. Do not just go over backward into a possible broken back.

This is a mighty tough trick to master and do gracefully, but it can be a really sensational accomplishment.

**Dick Borello falling out of a Handstand into a Billy Keen Drag**

205

## THE JIMMY RICHARDSON LAYOUT

In the realm of strong-arm or muscle-grinding feats this bit of riding skill is outstanding.

Don't get me wrong. This is a hard trick but — like the Elder Drag Layout No. 96 — it takes more strength than riding ability. The timing or balance or acrobatic maneuvers that are important in other stunts are of little use here.

To hold the body straight out from the side of the horse while hanging by the hands and supported by the neck and shoulders and then to pull oneself back to the saddle takes a great deal of exertion. So much, in fact, that this trick is very rarely seen. This is a challenge that can lead to a lot of hard work before it is mastered.

Besides the originator I know of two fellows, Ralph Clark and Tommy Cropper, who used to try to out do each other in performing this stunt on the Ringling Bros. and Barnum and Bailey Circus when we toured with them in 1938.

The trick is started a good deal like No. 47, the Side Stand Neck Straddle. The big difference is the handholds which must be long enough to allow the rider's head to go beneath the horse.

Just try this. Raise your left leg and move it over the rear of the saddle to the right side. With the right hand thumb down holding the saddlehorn, the left palm up holding the left crupper handhold you lean over the saddle. Let yourself down to full arms' length as you kick the right leg free of the stirrup. Both legs should be up in a vertical position now. Try to get a great deal of support from the head and shoulders since you want your legs to continue out until they and your body are at right angles to the horse and parallel to the ground.

← START

This is the position to hold, and, when you are ready, raise the legs back up to a vertical position. From here it is a matter of choice. You can split your legs to land astride either the rump or the neck.

If you have done this while your horse was standing still, the chances are ten to one that you failed to complete the trick. Did the saddle turn because it was not cinched tightly enough? Or did your neck and stomach muscles give out? No matter. Now you will know what to do. The pickup strap from the forks of the saddle will allow you to adjust the length for your correct arm reach.

A rear saddle string or strap from the crupper handhold will give you the same aid for the left arm. It is quite important that your body be down low enough on the side of the horse to reach a fairly comfortable position.

If you were very fortunate and had long arms plus a horse with a small barrel, the saddlehorn and crupper handholds we described first were ideal for you. If not, a little experimenting with the straps, plus a lot of neck-twisting and muscle-cramping exertion will lead to complete and well-earned mastery of the trick.

There is one very odd thing about trick riding. What may be extremely difficult for me may be quite easy for you. We never know until we try.

**The Richardson Layout done by George Pitman**

207

## TAILSTAND TO A BILLY KEEN DRAG

We know you are not going to try this before you learn the Billy Keen Drag No. 94 and the Tailstand No. 45.

With these two for a starter, it is quite simple to describe how to do them in combination.

The rider holds the Tailstand position until ready to go into the Drag. Now the legs are quickly doubled up tightly, and, as the horse lifts or rises in his stride, the legs are jerked straight up. This combined lift raises the rider's head and shoulders far enough to enable him to roll with his head out, into the Drag.

If you could see this done I know you would like it.

← START

Ken Williams Doing a Tail Stand

Paul St. Croix
doing a Billy Keen Drag

## THE CROSSOVER ROLL

**The Crossover Roll done by Smokey Chism at Cheyenne Frontier Days**

This is a "Smokey" Chism origination, and, though it is different, you will note the resemblance to a Crossover Horn Cartwheel.

The rider grasps the horn in both hands, does a half Horn Spin to the neck of the horse to the starting position of this trick. Then he drops off to the horse's left by twisting to the left to allow the body to face forward as the left leg comes off the neck.

When his feet hit the ground the rider turns outward and pushes with his feet to lift over the horse to the other side. Going over the saddle the rider is "belly" up.

Now on the right side of the horse, the rider continues down facing the rear until his feet touch the ground. Getting a lift from this, the rider rises toward the rear "belly" up, and turns over in the air to land back in his starting position on the neck.

← START

# THE CHEYENNE CROSSOVER

This trick picked up the "Cheyenne" tag because it was performed first at the "Daddy of them all", the Cheyenne Frontier Days, in 1948.

The trick riders were discussing various unusual tricks and the writer said that he just got an idea for what he thought could be another unusual one.

That afternoon, during the trick riding event, he went ahead and successfully demonstrated the trick.

Part of the stunt is similar to the Somersault Through the Seat of the Saddle No. 65, but this has an entirely new start.

The rider grasps the horn with his right hand, thumb down, rests his left on top of it, and carries his left leg back over the saddle to be alongside his right leg. The left hand now goes to the left crupper handhold.

With these two grips the rider kicks his foot from the stirrup and drops to the ground alongside the horse. His body is facing the horse, therefore to get the lift to carry him up and over, he must hit the ground well ahead of the withers. This distance is important for, if the rider's body is too close, it will be hung up against the left arm.

With this lift, the rider, facing the horse, does a high somersault up and over the saddle, to a dive out at right angles to the left side of the horse.

← START

Going straight between his arms in this way the rider's feet touch the ground at the left of the horse facing outward. He turns his body toward the rear, kicks himself away from the ground into a tuck to land astride the neck facing the rear.

If you do a Saddle Somersault No. 65, there is no reason why you can't add the variations. A little time spent with these will add a great deal to the value of your routine. If you are working a number of performances at a fair or rodeo, it is possible to use these changes to vary your runs from show to show, or perhaps someone else in the group is doing a similar trick and you will want to show a different way to do it.

## 141

## REVERSE CRUPPER TO BACKWARD STAND IN THE SADDLE

This is another variation of a Reverse Crupper No. 85. This one requires a tremendous "lift" to allow a rider to gain the necessary height.

Sitting backward in the saddle, the rider takes the left crupper handhold with his left hand palm up. The right hand now crosses over the left arm to the right crupper palm down, knuckles facing forward. Leaning forward the rider raises his legs above the saddle, brings them together toward the left side of the horse, and drops to the ground. On the way down the body is twisted to the left, allowing both feet to reach the ground with the toes pointed toward the horse's head. The rider hits the ground, tucks and springs upward, turning toward the horse as the feet sail upward toward the saddle.

Now, here, instead of spreading the legs as usual, as the rider turns over in the air, they are kept together in the tuck to allow the feet to land in the seat of the saddle. This puts the rider in a backward position in the saddle and he can go into No. 14, the Backward Crouch Stand, or some other trick of his choice. That's what makes trick riding such an attractive challenge. You can vary the combinations for added zest just as easily as a chef adds his spices to change the flavor of the food.

← ◄◄◄ START

## THE TAIL RIDE

This ride has one definite and singular feature. It is the end. That is, it is as far as a rider can go toward the rear of the horse and ride with both hands free. This feat and the following one, the Head Ride, prove that trick riders will ride anywhere and everywhere on a horse. Perhaps the only reason they haven't gone further is they just ran out of horse!

Well, you will want to know how to ride on the tail of your horse now even though you never intend to do a comedy routine and read a newspaper while you do it.

The *modus operandi* is this: Tie a large dowel or tree branch about one and one-half or two inches in diameter into the horse's tail. This stick should be from 12 to 16 inches in length.

To fasten the stick securely you can either tie a knot in the tail or divide the tail hair in two equal parts as you would to tie the knot, but instead wrap the hair around the stick and lay the remainder up above to be fastened securely to the rest of the tail with a narrow strap tightly buckled around it.

Both of these methods have been used, but either can slip if loosely tied. Try it while the horse is standing first!

You don't want to be left sitting red-faced in the dust as your horse continues running blithely down the track.

When the stick is in place, the rider slides back over the rump, holding the crupper handholds, to a straddled position over the horse's tail. The stick will be high up across the thighs with the rider's legs spread just outside the horse's legs.

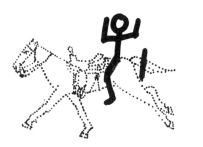 

212

When the rider feels secure he lets loose with both hands and raises them.

To return to the saddle, the crupper handholds are grasped to allow the rider to pull up out of the Tail Ride.

For the horse's sake, the rider should be fairly light in weight. No one likes a tailless horse.

**The Tail Ride as done by Dick Borello**

← START

213

## THE HEAD RIDE

Like our preceding trick this is as far as you go, but in the opposite direction. This, too, would be an ideal trick for a small, light-weight rider.

The midget Cucola, with the famous circus rosinback riding troupe, the Zoppe-Zavattas, always got a laugh from his version of this trick.

To accomplish it, the rider, sitting backward on the horse's neck, both hands on the horn, pushes himself almost to the ears of the horse and then reaches back with his legs to cross them over the face of the horse. This must be done carefully to keep from hitting the horse in the eyes, or otherwise making him headshy.

Obviously, to return, the rider releases his leg grip and slides back toward the horn pulling himself ahead with the aid of the horn handhold.

← START

**The Head Ride**

## SPIN FROM THE RUMP TO THE NECK

This is a good, showy method of going from a sitting position on the rump to a face-forward position astride the neck of the horse. There are much easier ways of getting to the neck of the horse. When you finish this procedure, however, you will feel good, for you will have done a simple but complicated-looking maneuver.

To start the trick you must be sitting behind the saddle. Perhaps you have just finished doing a Crupper Jump and want to go to the neck for a series of Neck Scissors. Grasp the saddlehorn with the right hand, thumb down, the left holds the cantle or a crupper handhold. Leaning forward, the legs are brought over to the right side of the horse. You will now be sitting sideways with the two handholds. Hold yourself up straight as your legs slide down and you swing forward. Then turn the body to the left to allow the left leg to be raised over the neck of the horse in front of the saddlehorn.

The body is in a half twist here. Turn loose the left hand and grasp the horse's mane to help pull yourself around to the forward position on the neck.

Neck Scissors No. 39 or Scotty Black's Spread-eagle Drag No. 131 can be used as follow up tricks from this position. And, if you don't like the position, just reverse the action and return to the rump.

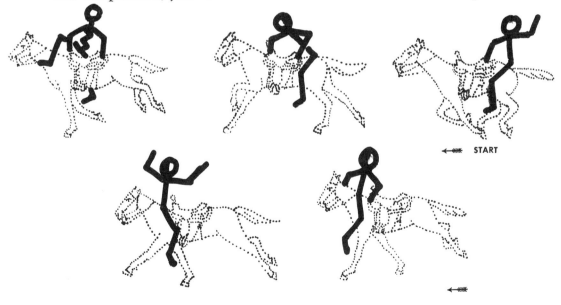

START

## 8. TRICK RIDING UNLIMITED

ALL OF THE PRECEDING TRICKS and their combinations are only a part of the great variety of riding stunts possible. Perhaps you would like to strike out on another tangent with your trick-riding ability. Maybe you have two or more horses you would like to ride at once. Perhaps there are two co-operating trickriders and only one horse.

At any rate, if you have mastered trick riding on one horse there is no reason whatsoever for your not being able to go on to greater glory and fun by adding other skills.

We have mentioned the use of props, the added features, carrying a flag, spinning a rope, etc. This field is wide open. Midge McLain does the Cossack Drag with an American flag tied to her upright foot. A Russian Cossack did the "Possum Belly" ride while playing a concertina and another did vaults with his head and body enclosed in a sack tied around his waist. The author did a Saddle Somersault with his head enclosed in a sack and a girl rider went under her horse's belly while blindfolded.

These feats illustrate the extra touch some riders add to standard features.

**This is a perfect trick to perform on the Fourth of July or when there are other riders doing the Hippodrome Stand**

Another trend in trick riding is the comedy variation. Clowns at rodeos, Ty Stokes, Ed Bowman, Pinky Gist, Slim Pickens, Tin Horn Hank Keenan, Billy Keen, and Andy Womack, added laugh-producers to their tricks.

They would lose their pants while vaulting or doing the Tail Drag, sit backward reading a newspaper, do a Hooker Arm Drag while carrying a suitcase that accidentally (?) came open to spread its weird contents the length of the track, or ride with their feet in the hippodrome strap while seated in a chair. These clowns would do anything for a laugh.

**Ann and Byron Hendrix in their comedy Roman riding act**

217

Going on to another popular branch of trick riding there are the double stunts. Many of the tricks can be done by two people working at the same time on the same horse. The photos illustrate a few of these. You can work out many interesting ideas. Dick Griffith and another trickrider on the 101 Ranch Wild West Show once tried a double vault both using the same horn. The idea was for Dick to go high over the horse and the other rider just to skim through the saddle.

Standing in a stirrup on each side, holding onto the extra long horn the boys started the horse. At a signal they both dropped off to vault over. But, and here's the payoff, one got mixed up and forgot if he was to go high or low! It was just a tangled mass of arms and legs as they met above the horse in a climax which was hilariously funny to everyone else.

These double stunts have quite often ended, in practice, in an unpredictable manner. So, be forewarned, work them out throughly before attempting them on a running horse.

The Cossacks probably have the distinction of originating the largest mass riding stunt done on one horse. They call this "The Feast Table Ride." Four men ride on one horse! One is backward on the neck, usually playing a concertina, two others stand in the stirrups on each side waving bottles and holding a square board or table top between them, and the fourth rides sitting forward behind the saddle!

218

Smokey and Sunbeam Chism double trick riding. Sunbeam doing a Layover the Neck and Smokey doing a Ted Elder Drag

Paul and Marie St. Croix in a double trick-riding stunt

219

The two stirrup riders each have a leg extended across the saddle for the opposite rider to sit astride thereby "locking" them in place enabling them to ride free-handed.

The nearest thing to this so far attempted by rodeo riders has been the three-girl stunt done some years ago at Salinas, California. Two girls did Russian Drags from opposite sides of the horse while a third did a Back Drag over the tail.

Harvey and Mildred Red doing a double Spread Eagle Shoulder Carry. See also frontis showing Deans in a double trick

From here now it is only a short step to Pyramid Riding or Roman Riding.

In Roman Riding, riders have straddled three horses and ridden with their feet on two outer horses on a *five* horse team! Fred Weiderman of the Buffalo Bill Wild West Show accomplished this sensational and never equalled feat.

**Louie Cabral jumping three horses over a fire jump**

There have been other great Roman riders who did the almost impossible. To quote from an article in the *Horse and Horseman* Magazine of August, 1936, about Colonel Frank K. Hyatt of Penn. Military College: "In 1909, Capt. Hyatt rode standing up across the parade ground adding to his team of horses each time. He rode up to nine and then reversed to ride them in a backward position. Then went on to finish riding a grand total of 17 horses." The photo accompanying the article showed him above 7 horses straddling one.

Riding Roman over jumps or trick riding over jumps has also proved a fatal fascination to horsemen. Elenor Gettsander in 1936 at Iowa's Championship Rodeo in Sidney, Iowa, did a routine of trick-riding stunts over the jumps. Another unfortunate girl, at a rodeo in Colorado, tried going under her horse's belly over the jumps and hit her head on the bar and was killed.

You can make trick riding as dangerous as you like. You set your own limit.

**Byron Hendricks doing a Shoulder Stand on Roman team**

**Lee Hendricks doing a Free Stand while jumping two "free" horses**

Little Sandra Sue Strauss, with a foot on each outside pony, is spread so wide as to be hardly visible above her hurdle-jumping steeds

The Hendricks twins, familiar sights at the Madison Square Garden Rodeo, are shown here performing their criss-cross, Roman standing riding, car hurdle at a rodeo in Texas

Lee Hendricks does an almost unbelievable jump through a hoop and pirouettes in the air to land backward with one foot on each horse. This agile rodeo horseman then repeats the spinning jump to return to his original forward position on the horses

Always the thrill-seeker, Lou Cabral, has surpassed all his preceding accomplishments by training the upredictable Brahma to leap a spear-topped hurdle while he stands straight on their backs

224

## 9. A WORD TO THE WISE

*These are the tricks and the way they are done. However, there is a little more to trick-riding than merely knowing the methods.* Clothing is important, background or foundation training helps, a comfortable method of taking spills is invaluable, and it is nice to know how to sell your skill if you wish.

### CLOTHING

Clothing should be close fitting and sturdy. Under extenuating circumstances men have done trick riding in fantastic costumes such as rubber hip boots, a slicker and chaps, but they would be the first to say it was not satisfactory.

Trixie McCormick doing the Backdrag, giving you a clear view of the foot straps she used in performing this trick at the Red Bluff, California, Rodeo. Note her tight-fitting outfit

The original Russian Cossacks did their riding complete with caracul fur hat, long military coat, ornate dagger swinging from the belt (and some even carried a saber between their teeth.) Of the original group who came to the United States four met a gruesome death because of this billowy uniform.

Benefit by the experience of these Cossacks and wear shirts and saddle pants that allow freedom of action but do not float about to catch on the equipment. Girls who do only the simple top tricks can sometimes wear full blouses but difficult tricks can easily end in catastrophe in such a costume.

Note the various styles of wardrobe worn by this group of trick riders at the Salinas California Rodeo. This famous rodeo always features an outstanding trick riding event

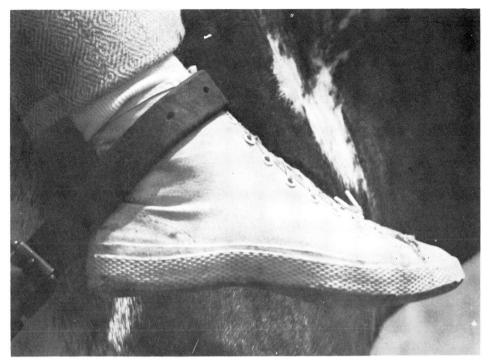

Simple tennis shoes are worn by many trick riders although an increasingly large number are adopting a high topped shoe with crepe rubber sole. This gives some support to the ankles, looks well, and as the shoes are made to order they can come in whatever color you desire. Companies that make ice-skating shoes do a very nice job on these trick-riding shoes, since all their styles provide ideal ankle support. Boots are seldom worn by trick riders except for parade purposes.

The use of a hat nowadays is purely arbitrary. Most riders cannot keep a hat on when they are working and after reading about the tricks you can easily see why. Some feel that a hat adds sufficiently to the appearance of the act to juggle it on the finish tricks, but when beginning it's really a bother. Some contest rules in the past, with appearance in mind, required the contestant to wear a hat during the event. (Viz. the Tex Austin Rodeo in Hollywood, 1935.)

Guards are necessary only if you have special weaknesses or are doing tricks which tend to give you a beating. Some women trick riders wear a leather guard under their blouses if they do shoulder stands on a high-headed horse that drives them into the horn. Wrist guards or bands are frequently used for support. Ankle bands are used for the same reason if high topped shoes are not worn.

A suprisingly large number of trick riders claim to have a "Bum Knee" and they wear a rubber sleeve on it. For some unknown reason this is usually the left knee.

A — CLOTHES FOR PRACTICE

1—No hat and no gloves.

2—A turtle-neck sweater or tight fitting sweat shirt is perfect. Wear something that does not bind or inhibit freedom of action yet will not catch on the horn or other parts of the saddle. Remember in case of a fall you want to be covered with some protection.

3—Blue jeans or Levis are fine. Do not, however, wear them so tight that you have difficulty moving.

4—Tennis shoes are excellent. Any rubber soled shoe will do but the high tops give more ankle support and are preferred for this reason.

5—Wear guards on any part of you that is falling apart. Do not wear them as a preventive measure. They get in the way, and so should be ignored unless you actually need them.

B — CLOTHES FOR SHOW

1—If you must wear a hat be sure it is neat, clean, blocked and that is goes well with your color scheme. Avoid brown. It will look dirty to an audience. No gloves.

2—Wear a shirt or blouse that is comfortable to work in and colorful enough to please the audience. Select the colors that look well on you and will stand out from the horse. A perfect job of camouflaging is to wear white on a white horse, etc.

3—Trousers should be of the saddle-pants type, well built, and either match the shirt or blend well with it. It is not wise to cut yourself in half with contrasting colors. Men and women teams should wear similar looking clothes. The riding skirt or divided skirt is generally a washout as far as trick riding is concerned.

4—If you wear tennis shoes, be sure they are clean, white, and without holes. Wear white socks too. If you wear high-topped shoes, have them made in the same colors as your clothes or whiten them. Wear a strap from the cuffs of the pants under your foot to hold your pant legs down. It does not matter if your legs are knotted and hairy or perfectly beautiful, bare legs detract from trick riding.

5—If you wear a guard keep it hidden or as obscure as possible. The public likes to think its athletes are in perfect shape. Do not disillusion the public by looking as though you are held together by leather straps, rubber bands, and bits of baling wire.

# BACKGROUND WORK

To a large extent the quality of trick riding could be improved, the length of time a man is "tops" could be lengthened, and a great many guards could be eliminated, if trick riders spent a little more time in foundation training.

Most of us started trick riding because we were restless just sitting in the saddle all the time. We began climbing around on the horse just for the fun of it, saw someone who could really trickride, and decided to copy him. We learned from watching a finished trick and from inventing our own — a depressingly slow and inferior method. We went at it backwards and although we have accomplished some tricks which come close to the impossible, we could have been better if we had prepared for trick riding in the beginning.

**Nancy Bragg's Backbend shows acrobatic skill**

The new serious trick riders are going about this in a businesslike manner. It often brings a look of disdain from the old timers but it definitely pays off. It took a long time for Buff Brady to admit that he studied ballet all one summer. It sounded a little funny to the boys around the chutes. But Brady can do a One-Foot Knife-Split standing on the back of a galloping horse! The rest of us do not feel like trying it for the simple reason that we cannot even do it on the ground with someone holding us up. The trick is Brady's because he knows ballet. Don't laugh. Try it!

**Sunbeam Sky Eagle shows the benefit of acrobatic training with her neat splits to the horse's neck**

The clean Vaults, Cartwheels that look like a Cartwheel, Splits to the Neck that are as neat as an acrobat's back flip — they are the results of training in acrobatics and tumbling. The good trick riders do not reach their perfect form by either accident or pure genius. They trained for it on the ground in schools, colleges, sport centers, and circuses where an expert could yell at them "Keep your feet together! I said *tuck*, not tie one shoelace!"

Acrobatics require perfect timing, co-ordination, quick reflexes, and exact form. Ballet teaches the same physical unity of action with a different type of expression. Both acrobats and ballet dancers have

230

tackled trick riding even when they did not have the vaguest idea of how to handle a horse.

Besides the excellent foundation training of these two fields, the warming-up exercises which they teach should also be adopted by trick riders. The exercises give muscle tone, elasticity, and the peak of physical efficiency. Experiments have shown that a trick rider who goes into his routine cold will expend approximately eight times more energy than a rider who goes into a similar routine with the advantage of a ballet-learned warm-up.

No wonder the unprepared burn out. No wonder their joints ache, not from injury or damp weather, but from strain. Muscles were pulled harder than necessary because they were slow to start moving; the heart had to go into action too suddenly. This is not a discourse on physiology, but with a knowledge of some ballet warm-up exercises you will be a better and healthier trick rider. Whether you are a man, woman, boy, or girl, stop turning up your nose and get in shape. If you ride professionally you will put on a better show. If you trickride for the fun of it, you will have more fun. Get the sleep out of your muscles. Try these ballet exercises.

1—*Plier* (pronounced Pleeay) This is a deep knee bend. Hold a support of some kind with the left hand and holding your back very straight, bend your knees until you are almost sitting on your ankles. Then rise to a standing position again. These are to be done very slowly to get the benefit of the stretching to the muscles. About ten are sufficient. Remember to keep your back straight and head up.

2—*Kicks.* Hold something such as a door knob, fence post, or stall door which is at shoulder height. Kick high to the front about five times. Next kick to the side, and then to the back. Turn around and do the same kicks with the other leg. Do not allow the leg to bend at the knee. Keep the toe pointed even though it hurts a little.

3—*Développé.* Turn your left foot to point directly left and your right foot to point directly right. Now bring your feet together with the right foot in front of the left. Now take your right foot and lift it up with toe pointed, to follow against your left leg until you reach the

**Faye Blessing shows the relationship between ballet and trick riding**

knee. This will stretch those muscles! Change the position and do the same thing with the left leg.

4—*Ronde-Jambe.* Follow the *Développé* by putting your leg out in front of you until the leg is straight and slowly bring it around your body, to the right, until it is straight out in back. Do this combination slowly and remember to keep your back straight, head up, and leg stiff. After doing this with the right leg, turn around and do the same with the left. It will make the muscles ache at first but it unties the knots (and, incidentally, will prevent bunchy muscles from developing in the legs of women trick riders.)

This warming up is important. If you can, observe the circus performers loosening up before their turns, when next you visit a circus. They know the value of the exercises, these ground tumblers, rosin-back performers, flyers, catchers, top mounters, and understanders. In the circus, too, you will see additional evidence of the value of this as a habit. Occasionally you will be able to catch acrobats over 60 years of age still doing their round-off, flip flop, and back somersault!

Sports such as swimming, ice-skating, or tennis will help keep the body alert and maintain tone. Most trick riders like to keep to their field, however, and so it is recommended that you take up rosin-back riding for the same effect. Work on the bare-back horse will teach you a good deal about balance, vaults, and acrobatics as applied to a moving base. If you have the time and the opportunity by all means learn rosin-back riding. Among other things, you can learn to fall.

You have further to fall from a rosin-back horse than from a trick-riding horse, but there is time on that slow canter to study the art of falling. And it is an art. You can fall and break an arm or you can fall very comfortably and roll to your feet, a little dusty but none the worse for wear.

Learn to double up as you fall so that you will land with your head, arms, and legs, tucked inside. You will hit the earth first with the back of your right shoulder, and roll easily from there. Try to hold onto the horse and catch something with your hands enough to be able to vault back to the saddle. But when you are actually torn loose, double up quickly and roll when you strike the ground. No matter what position you fall from, you can double so that it is your shoulders that take the blow and not your head or arms.

With that method the problem of broken arms and legs is practically eliminated. Duck your head, hit on the right shoulder and roll. It is very simple, painless, and valuable. You can even practice falling until it becomes automatic.

The possibility of falling is always before the trick rider and so he must figure ways to get free from strap tricks, a way to fall into the saddle—or a way to break the fall until he can catch some part of the horse with his hands in order to recover with a vault. And if torn loose and none of these will work, he must be prepared to take the fall without being hurt.

Your horse can help a good deal in both preventing falls and in making them easier, more comfortable. To do this he needs to know you, the tricks, and to be genuinely interested in both. Never whip or beat your horse after you have fallen. Even if it was his fault, wait until he makes the mistake which unloaded you and then go after him. As what he has done is probably merely a mistake and not pure viciousness, it is not recommended that the horse ever be whipped. As you rise, dirty and mussed from a fall, your temper is very likely to be on fire. Don't take it out on the horse. If you do he will be so frightened the next time he feels you slip that he may lose his head and really smash you up.

Not only can your horse help prevent falls, he can save your life if you are hung up and dragging. He will learn from experience to consider himself something of a juggler, especially for Stands. Although he will keep going straight, an experienced horse will often put in a little roll to his gait to shift his slightly off-balance rider back to center.

Horses have been known to do everything but tie their legs in knots to keep from stepping on a fallen rider. Well-trained horses will almost always come back to check and see if the fallen rider is hurt, and then when the rider gets up in one piece, go trotting off in high glee over the whole thing. And should the rider be seriously hurt, they will almost always stand by to watch, if not actually with sympathy, at least with curiosity.

A green horse will lose his head if the rider drags. It will scare him and he may go crazy, run like a mad thing without direction—even to the point of crashing through a fence. An experienced trick-riding horse is quite familar with what should be going on from his rider; and, strangely enough, even though he has been taught always to keep running, in the case of an accidental hangup, he will sometimes stop.

There are many good books on horse-training and for the new trick rider it is worth while to study them. There are many times in trick riding when your very life depends upon your horse. Know him and his idiosyncrasies. Treat him well and do it right.

Care for your horse is fairly standard wherever you are. Trick-riding horses work very hard even if it is only for short periods. They should be groomed thoroughly every day, unless you do not mind getting a face full of dust. Your horse should be grained. Feed whole oats, at least two quarts a day. Enough hay to satisfy his hunger and keep him sleek and fat. Do not overfeed as a roly-poly is not ideal; but keep the horse well filled-out.

Show work requires a certain type of equipment which for clarity will be listed with approximate costs. Besides this equipment you will need to have your horse checked regularly by a veterinarian for teeth, legs, and worms. The horse will need a shot for *encephalomyelitis* (sleeping sickness) once a season.

**Dorothy Herbert doing a Fire Jump while blindfolded**

## EQUIPMENT

1 — *Trick riding saddle*—Costs vary. Check with manufacturers. Saddles are now being decorated or completely covered with plastic of different colors which is excellent for show work. It is easy to clean, always bright, scratches and scuffs do not show. The all-white quilted leather saddles are the most popular, although they require more care than the plastic ones.

2 — *Bridle and breast collar.* A bridle and bit, plus the optional breast collar can be reasonable or expensive depending on their use, for work or show purposes.

3 — You will need a cooler blanket, heavy blanket, curry comb and brush, two buckets, and a hay fork. This is the minimum.

4 — *Halter* — A good sewed halter is fine, but usually, rope halters with woolskin on the noseband are used. Being a much cheaper article they are seldom stolen. Two tie ropes of haltershanks about 8 foot in length will also be necessary.

5 — *A horse trailer* — Get one with tandem wheels and it is best if it can be enclosed. An open-air trailer exposes the horse too much and he will catch colds easily.

6 — *An automobile* — get a car that can pull a horse trailer safely and economically. Small cars often give more trouble than they are worth when put to such heavy work.

7 — Besides the cost of feed you will have to watch your horse's shoes and have them changed about every four weeks. Trick-riding horses need enough shoes to equip a debutante. Use rubber shoes if it is ever necessary to work on pavement, or on a stage. Have shoes with caulks in the heels if you are working on turf or on wet, slippery areas. For ordinary tracks light plates are the best as they give the horse the most satisfactory type of action.

# SUBSTITUTE EQUIPMENT

If you do not care to invest in the standard trick-riding equipment and would rather use what you have, here are some methods which you can apply.

*English Saddle* — It is not as secure as the Western type horn, but you can use the pommel of the saddle for a hand grip in vaulting. Place the left hand down with the fingers curving under the saddle and cover it with the right hand. With this grip you can do almost anything that is done on the standard trick-riding saddle. It will require a little more skill but it can be done.

For the Hippodrome Stand, cross the stirrup leathers across the seat of the saddle, put your feet in the stirrups, and stand up. The feet are not secured solidly, however, as they are in the regulation hippodrome strap.

The Slick Saddle Stand can be done by standing in the saddle using the reins for balance. Backward Stands should not be done on an English saddle.

The Russian Drags can be done by changing the girth or tying down the stirrup but the Fender Drag is done in exactly the same way. It may be slightly painful because the English stirrup leather is quite narrow compared to the Western.

Side Stands are done by holding the billet straps and are delightfully comfortable as there is no horn to miss.

Side Stands, Lay Overs, Balances are all done by holding the pommel and cantle of the saddle. Since there are no back-holds none of the Crupper Vaults or Tail Stands can be done. However, the Arabesques and various Sprinter's Stance tricks are easy.

*Bareback* — this is slightly difficult as there is nothing but the mane or reins actually handy to use for a hold. You can do many of the Vaults from the mane and can stand on the horse's back holding the reins. Of course a Free Stand is possible if you can do it at all.

Smokey Chism does a Shoulder Stand on a bareback horse by holding the horse's skin and long hair. He admits, however, that he can only do the trick in the winter time when the horse has a long coat.

**Smokey Chism doing Vaults or Overs with only a bareback rigging**

He also does a Crupper Vault bareback by holding to the horse's hip bones. As he is the only rider who can do these tricks consistently you need not develop an inferiority complex if you fail.

It goes without saying that none of the Drags are possible. However, if your balance is good both the Stances and Lay Overs are possible.

*Surcingle* — this will give you an even larger repertoire of tricks than the English saddle will allow. Your vaults will be a little toward the back and turn-over tricks will be difficult because of the way the handholds are placed. However, trick riding with a surcingle is very interesting and different from other types of trick riding. Many riders use it just for the fun of it, even though professionally they use a trick saddle because of its greater allowances.

Do not do any of the Drags on a surcingle unless it has a metal backpiece. A hold is easy to attach but the all-leather surcingle turns too easily and you will surely hang up sooner or later.

238

*Western Saddle* — This is just like a trick saddle and so can be fitted with most of the holds which the standard trick saddle has. Its drawbacks are the short horn which is difficult to grip, and the high cantle which is always in the way. Aside from these inconveniences, which are a serious problem in many tricks, the Western saddle comes as close as possible to the trick-riding saddle. Lay Over tricks will probably not be possible due to the narrowness of the seat. Aside from that, carry on!

If you are buying a saddle, get the trick-riding saddle. But if you already have a saddle and do not wish to buy another, you can use what you have in the aforementioned ways. You may be limited as to what you can do; but some trick riding can be done on any kind of mount and with any kind of gear.

**Any kind of mount or any kind of gear can be used. When only ten years of age, Betsy Ross went over a four-foot six-inch hurdle while doing the Cossack Stand**

Equipment and skill alone are not enough to get show work. Getting jobs is sometimes more painful than preparing for them—and certainly more difficult than actually working. Putting on an act is a cinch compared to the problems of getting the job.

This is not so much because work for trick riders is hard to find. It is because most riders are not good at handling their own publicity or at writing a letter that sells. As almost all work must be obtained via a letter, trick riders shudder with horror and then sit down and try to describe themselves and their work. Unless you know the ropes, and write selling letters with considerable ease and fluency, you may have difficulty. Therefore we present a few tips for the newcomer to the field.

Practice about ten tricks that will photograph well and are unusual. Learn to do them as combination runs whenever possible. Omit the Fender Drag, Lay Overs, and Sprinter's Stance. These are too commonplace and ridiculously easy.

Select the ten tricks with an eye to their show value, photographic qualities, and difficulty. Then practice until your form is perfect. Next hire a photographer who knows how to take action shots, and get good clear pictures of each trick at the height of action. Wear show wardrobe and equipment. Work before a neutral background so that the trick can be clearly seen.

Design a letter head with the photographs reduced in size and artistically distributed, featuring the best trick. Include on the letterhead your name and permanent address with telephone number.

Start your letter in business style with the date to the right; the name of the show manager, street address, city and state, on separate lines to the far left. Make your letter brief, to the point, and complete. Explain that you are a trick rider and that your planned itinerary will take you within the vicinity of the show with an open date. Present your qualifications by listing the tricks which you do, referring to the pictures in the letterhead. Request that you be hired by the trick and state what salary you want for this performance. Close the letter with a request to hear as soon as possible about the possibility of your employment.

To find show dates, look in the *Amusement Business* Magazine, especially the Spring Special issue for the lengthy fair list. *Rodeo News*, Paul's Valley, Oklahoma and *Rodeo Sport News* published by the Rodeo Cowboys Association, Inc., at 2929 West 19th Avenue, Denver, Colorado 80204 carry Rodeo information. *Hoofs and Horns* and *Western Horsemen* magazines carry additional Rodeo and horse show data.

Figure a route which would keep you working almost every day with short drives between shows and then sit down to concoct a letter that will sell you to the managers. Write to far more shows than you can possibly play. They will not all hire you and you increase your chances of working steadily by making many applications.

The *Amusement Business* can be picked up at almost any newsstand or magazine stand. It carries a complete list of fair dates and the routes of circuses. From the *American Horsemen-Sportologue* you will get the list of society horse shows. These fields are just as pleasant to work as rodeos and often pay more.

**Chief Cabral, a former motion picture stunt man, rodeo bucking horse rider, big city fireman, etc., has an insatiable appetite for thrills.**

241

In the Middle West almost every county has a fair. Naturally the larger fairs will pay the most but you can often fill in with the little ones. Horse shows seldom hire more than one trick rider at a time and so you will have to work harder in a horse show, making at least eight runs with good ricks. Trick riders have almost spoiled this field by turning lazy, running about three tricks and disappearing to the stables to collect the check. Keep in mind that the Society Horse Show is run by wealthy people and that a good reputation with them will pay off, too.

Where rodeos, fairs, and horse shows may hire you for a week or less, a circus will take on trick riders for a complete season. This is good, steady work but also requires special equipment in that you must have a trailer to live in while traveling with a motorized circus. Circuses usually hire during the winter months or through January and February. The season may begin in the middle of March and continue until October. It is difficult to get a job with a circus after the show has opened and is on the road, although it never hurts to try.

For all jobs in show business remember that publicity is very, very important. Show business depends upon public support and the public comes to see the famous, the best, and the greatest. If the public does not know you even exist, your name has no drawing power. Show managers are interested in riders who will bring in the public. Therefore get your name and picture in the papers and magazines. Get every line of publicity possible. Don't forget to mention important work you have done such as stunt work for moving pictures, big shows such as Madison Square Garden, the American Royal, the Pendelton Rodeo, the Cow Palace, or Ringling Bros. Circus.

If you have been in a movie be sure to name it. If you have been sent abroad to Europe, the Hawaiian Islands, the Philippines, the Far East, Canada, or Mexico, be sure to mention it. And, incidentally, the foreign field is a good one if you are paid enough money or given a a long enough season to cover traveling expenses. England and Australia always like American trick riders as they have nothing similar. Russia, of course, has its Cossacks which are good, but the U.S. State

Department at this time frowns upon a trip to that country. If you can make foreign work pay, by all means take it. It will be good experience for you and show-managers at home dote on a rider with a foreign background.

A word aside here to show-managers. You will save your name, your riders, and put on better shows if you will hire by the trick. This business of hiring World Champion trick riders, without specifying that they do the tricks for which they are famous, is foolish. Any child can do a Hippodrome Stand, a One Hand Fender Drag, and a Sprinter's Stance. Hire riders by the tricks—by their good tricks!

And, to the man who is interested in trick riding only as a spectator, study the tricks carefully. You will feel as though you are actually participating when you know how the stunts are done. You will appreciate the performance more. You will know that trick riders are human beings and not supermonkeys. Knowing the dangers, the chances that are taken to do the tricks, you will like and respect the riders.

Some trick riders are quiet. Some are talkative. Some are lithe and graceful and a few are chunky. Most seem shy when not on horseback or at least talking about horses. All of them have a hundred stories to tell. All of them have a favorite trick they like to do and one they definitely like to avoid.

All-in-all they are a pretty swell bunch of folks and they take pride in their work. But don't think for one moment that they don't enjoy themselves!

You can, too. Now that you have finished reading and studying this book, get up, stretch, grab your Stetson, head for the corral and get your horse.

Once you start to trickride we *know* you'll like it.

## 10. TRICK RIDING FACTS — STRANGE BUT TRUE

TRICK RIDERS, although noted for their color and glamor around the rodeo circuit, are rugged individuals, rivaling the bronc rider for dried-rawhide and barbed-wire toughness.

Bronc-riding Champ Perry Ivory, who was once featured in Ripley's "Believe It Or Not", rode in the Salinas rodeo finals to win, riding with his broken leg in a cast. Not so fortunate was Ted Baker, who tried the same thing in 1934 at a rodeo in Oregon. He bucked off breaking his cast and rebreaking the leg.

Tales of the rodeo arena are studded with these examples of guts and ruggedness.

The trick riders, too, are found sharing this disregard of injury. Dick Griffith's ankles, feet, and wrists were so often injured that to dull the pain he would apply a freezing application of ether and kept up his sensational trick riding. This meant, of course, it would take much longer for the arm or leg to get well — but during that time *Dick was trickriding.*

One of the oddest of these trick-riding accounts concerns Walt Heacock's defiant acceptance of an injury's challenge. At Filer, Idaho, Walt's right arm was so inflamed from blood poisoning, it hung useless. Walt was determined to trickride at the rodeo and ignored all advice against it. He knew he could do a few top tricks plus some ground stunts using his good left hand, but he had a terrible problem. How was he going to keep the pain-racked, throbbing but useless, right arm out of his way?

The close observers in the rodeo audience probably wondered why one trick rider did his Vaults and Cartwheels with his right hand strapped to the saddle horn. They didn't know, but Walt did. *He wanted to trickride.*

In the past employment on the Wild West shows provided many cowboys with an "earn while you learn" existence. Many of rodeo's Greats—plus Movieland's Tom Mix, Buck Jones, and Will Rogers—got their start in this way. One of these budding rodeo champions was the almost legendary trick rider, Ted "Suicide" Elder. His prelude to stardom in 1926 was spent on the Ringling Bros., Barnum and Bailey Circus in the Wild West aftershow. His goal was already set. He was determined to win the World's Championship in Trick and Fancy Riding that Fall at the Madison Square Garden rodeo. He'd try any bizarre stunt suggested by his pals if it sounded at all possible. And what he thought possible was unbelievable. In previous years, on other shows, he had already accomplished every known trick. Now he was trying add new routines that would definitely eliminate all competition.

He originated the Cartwheels off the Horn, a Crupper Somersault to Forward on the Neck and his famous Tail Drag.

This Tail Drag he would practice when alone in the big top, since he wanted to keep it a secret from the other top riders on the show. They, too, had their eyes set on the championship. Ted had worked out all the details of this new creation to perfection when, of all the other trick riders on the show, who should invade his shroud of secrecy but Buff Brady. Buff, a real, typically rough, Son of . . . the West, never cared to practice, was afraid of nothing, and would tackle anything. Proof of this came during the next performance. He dove off the rear of his horse and did the Drag down past the amazed audience.

Think of the irony of this! The originator didn't know, until that moment, that his secret was out. His big triumph came later that year, however, since, he went on to win his coveted World's Championship at Madison Square Garden.

During the summer of 1932 the Al G. Barnes Circus featured Marco Borello in their Wild West aftershow. Twice a day, during both the afternoon and evening performances, Marco did the sensational feat of crawling between the hind legs of his trick-riding horse to climax the riding event.

The successful accomplishment of this phenomenal feat always came as a surprise to the unbelievers in the audience. But to a champion rider like Borello this was all in the day's work. The tables were turned, however, for one day his face also wore an amazed and surprised look at the finish of the trick.

Circus troupers know that few days pass without some unexpected event taking place on the lot. This particular day the unscheduled occurrence came during the trick-riding performance.

Borello was just passing through the hind legs of his running horse when it happened. The toes of both feet were still in the stirrups and he was face up beneath the horse reaching for the second handhold above the horse's tail. "Plop", with a dull thud Marco hit flat on his back on the ground beneath his horse. When he hit the ground he instinctively reached for the lost handhold, his hands clawing upward in a vain effort to reach the leather sling high above.

To the startled spectators he seemed to bounce as with a swish and a jerk he flew through the air to land back astride his horse!

While lying flat on the ground his groping hands had not searched in vain for the very tip of the flying tail was within his reach.

Before he had a chance to think, his speeding horse had jerked him into the air and onto it's back!

Yes, my friends, that day *he* was surprised.

*The End*

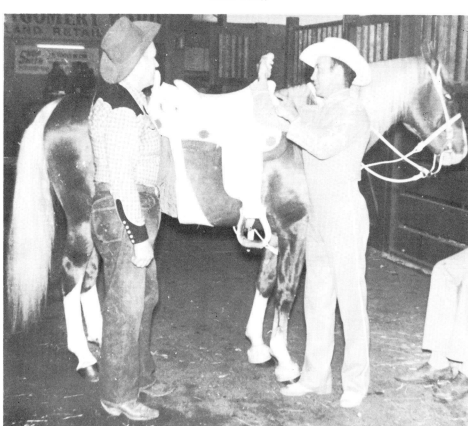

**Frank Dean and Dick Griffith discussing tricks for Frank's book. Photo taken at the Cow Palace at San Francisco**

246

# APPENDICES

## A. 144 BASIC TRICKS IDENTIFIED

In the following list the descriptions are brief and are intended only for identification purposes.

1—*The Horn Spin or Going Around the Horn.* Using both hands, the rider goes from the saddle to a backward position on the neck of the horse; then continues around the horn to return to the saddle.

2—*One-Hand Horn Spin.* Same as above only one hand is held overhead.

3—*No Hands Horn Spin or Free Horn Spin.* Same as preceding tricks but both hands are held overhead.

4—*One Half Lazyback or One Foot Layover the Saddle.* Rider sits sideways in the saddle, one foot in the stirrup, and leans back across the saddle with the other foot raised vertically.

5—*Lazyback or Layover the Saddle.* Rider is face up and on his back as in No. 4 but has both feet raised.

6—*Free Lazyback or Bee Ho Grey Back Balance.* Same as No. 5 but rider has his hands free and balances across the saddle in a horizontal position.

7—*Lazyback Roll Back.* Starts same as No. 5 but rider goes over backward touching the ground with his feet and then comes back.

8—*Half Upside Down on the Neck.* Rider has one foot in the stirrup, the other raised vertically as he lies face downward over the neck of his horse.

9—*Upside Down on the Neck.* Rider lies over one side of the horse's neck as in No. 8 but has *both* feet raised vertically.

10—*Layover the Neck.* The rider lies *face upward* over the neck of the horse, one foot in the stirrup and the other raised vertically.

11—*Layover the Neck to Vaults.* The rider starts as in No. 10 then raises *both* feet vertically, holds this position for a moment or so, then drops off into a vault to the saddle.

12—*Sprinter's Stance, or Crouch Stand in the Saddle.* Rider holds on with both hands as he stands sideways in the saddle with one foot raised upward.

13—*Sprinter's Crouch on the Rump.* Rider assumes the same position as No. 12 but faces forward in a stand on the horse's rump.

14—*Backward Sprinter's Stance.* Same position as No. 12 but rider stands *backward* with one foot in the saddle.

15—*Sprinter's Stance on the Neck.* Rider stands with one foot on the horse's neck, the other raised overhead, otherwise same as No. 12.

16—*Sprinter's Stance from the Withers.* Rider facing forward has one foot in a strap loop over the withers, the other is raised as high as possible.

17—*Backward Crouch Stand from the Withers.* Rider faces the rear, the raised foot being over the horse's head.

18—*Arabesque or One Knee Stand.* Rider gets behind saddle, balances on one knee and raises the other leg in the air.

19—*Half Fender Drag.* Rider facing the rear holds on to the horn with one hand and hangs off to the side of his horse, with one knee locked under the fender and stirrup leather, the other leg being free.

20—*Fender Drag.* Same as No. 19 but rider has both hands *free* and bends down toward the ground with both arms extended.

21—*Forward Fender Drag.* Rider facing forward squats on the side of the horse with the free leg extended straight forward beneath the stirrup leather.

22—*Faye Blackstone's Fender Drag.* Right foot in left stirrup, knee under stirrup leather, the rider squats alongside the side the horse facing forward with the left foot extended ahead. Rider has one rear handhold.

23—*Cossack, Russian, Suicide, or Death Drag.* Rider, with one foot in strap loop, hangs head downward over the saddle with the free foot raised above.

24—*Cossack Drag over the Neck.* Same as No. 23, but rider hangs down over neck, in front of the saddle horn with the free leg in front of the horse's chest.

25—*Death Drag Backward over the Neck.* Rider is facing the rear on the horse's neck when he goes into this version.

26—*Russian Drag Back of the Saddle.* Same as No. 23, but rider's secured leg is back of the cantle and rider hangs down behind the saddle.

27—*The Stroud Layout.* With one foot fastened high up, the other in the stirrup, the rider extends his body straight out in a horizontal position at right angles to the side of his horse.

28—*The Hippodrome, Liberty, or Cossack Stand.* The rider facing forward stands above the saddle with feet secured but hands free.

29—*Drunken Ride.* Same as No. 28, but rider weaves or leans from side to side, while waving a bottle in a simulated drunken stagger.

30—*Backward Hippodrome Stand.* Same as No. 28, but the rider stands facing the rear of the horse.

31—*Hippodrome Stand Back of the Cantle.* Same as No. 28, but the rider has his feet in loops at the rear of the saddle.

32—*The Jack Wright Drag.* The rider steps off to one side and lowers himself, with his free foot extended beneath his horse, till his pants pocket almost touches the ground.

33—*Stirrup Over the Horn Ride.* This drag is done when the rider's leg is placed in the loop formed when the stirrup is hooked over the saddlehorn.

34—*Indian Squat.* Rider sits close to the saddlehorn, crosses both legs over the horse's neck and raises both hands overhead.

35—*The George Hooker Arm Drag.* The rider hooks his elbow over the horn and runs alongside his horse, taking long, grotesque-looking, steps.

36—*Saddle Spin.* Rider turns around while seated in the saddle.

37—*Rump Spin.* Rider turns around while seated behind the saddle on the rump.

38—*Scissors in the Saddle.* The rider leans over, pushes his body into the air, crosses his legs and returns astride the saddle facing the opposite direction.

39—*Scissors on the Neck.* Similar to No. 38, except that the rider is astride the horse's neck and holds the saddle horn when doing the neck scissors.

40—*Scissors on the Rump or Hip Scissors.* Same as No. 38 except rider sits back on the rump.

41—*Crupper Scissors.* The rider drops off behind the horse and jumps back on, doing a scissors in the air to alight facing the rear.

42—*Back Drag.* The rider's feet are fastened over the rear jockeys of the saddle and he hangs down, face up, over the tail of the horse.

43—*The Harvey Rex Back Drag.* The rider's feet are fastened farther ahead than in No. 42 to allow him to lie on his stomach over the tail of the horse. Rex spins a rope in each hand while in this position.

44—*Midge McLain's Back Drag.* The rider lies back, face up, over the tail of the horse, one hand holds the crupper hand hold, the other, as Midge does it, spins a baton.

45—*Forward Tail Stand.* The rider is face down over the horse's tail with both feet raised perpendicularly.

46—*Backward Tail Stand.* Same as above, but the rider here faces backward and has his back instead of his chest against the horse.

47—*Side Stand Neck Straddle.* The rider, holding on from both the front and the rear of the saddle, goes face downward to a vertical stand against the side of the horse, then comes down sitting backward on the horse's neck.

48—*Single Vault or Pony Express Mount.* The rider, holding the saddle horn, jumps to the ground and vaults back astride the horse.

49—*Vault to Reverse in the Saddle.* Starts same as No. 48 but rider turns in the air to land backward on the horse. Both No. 48 or No. 49 are done to the saddle or to the rump.

50—*Double Vaults or Overs.* Same start as No. 48 but the rider keeps his legs together when he rises and goes completely over the horse to hit again on the opposite side, then returns, repeating these over and over.

51—*Hip or Crupper Vaults.* Using handholds at the rear of the saddle the rider vaults over the hips instead of over the saddle as in No. 50.

52—*The Outside Vault.* The rider turns his body *out* as he comes up from the ground and goes over or alights astride the saddle facing backward.

53—*One-Hand Vault.* Same as No. 48, except that the rider uses only one hand.

54—*Forward Vaults.* When doing this vault the rider raises his legs *forward* to cross over the horse's neck in *front* of the saddlehorn.

55—*Vaults and Splits to the Neck or Neck Splits.* The rider starts as in No. 48 but raises his legs over the saddlehorn to allow him to land astride the horse's neck in a backward position.

56—*Vault to the Neck with Both Feet on One Side.* Same as No. 55 but the feet are held together and turned to allow the rider to land sitting sideways on the neck of his horse.

57—*Neck Split Landing Forward on the Neck.* This is similar to No. 55, except that the rider crosses his legs when he splits them, and lands facing forward astride his horse's neck.

58—*Vault to Missing the Neck.* This starts the same as No. 56, but instead of landing in a sideways position on the neck of the horse, the rider misses it entirely.

59—*Vault Over the Neck to a Spin to the Saddle.* Same as No. 58 but the rider adds an outside spin, pivoting on the palm of his hand on the saddle horn, to return to the saddle.

60—*Saddle Splits.* Same as No. 55, but done from the rear of the saddle to allow the rider to land astride the saddle in a backward position.

61—*Shoulder Stand.* Rider is balanced on his shoulder, legs straight up, facing backward on the neck of his horse.

62—*Cantleboard Shoulder Stand.* The rider is balanced on his shoulder, legs straight up, but facing forward in his position behind the cantle of the saddle.

63—*Shoulder Stand in the Saddle.* The rider does this shoulder stand facing backward over the narrow part of the seat of the saddle.

64—*Backward Shoulder Stand in the Saddle.* The rider faces forward as he stands on his shoulder in the saddle.

65—*Saddle Somersault or Somersault Through the Seat of the Saddle.* The rider grasps both the front and rear of the saddle as he stands in one stirrup then dives over to strike the ground with his feet (facing the rear), then returns to the saddle or to the neck of his horse. Usually this somersault is done from a Sprinter's Stand No. 12.

66—*Forward Dive Off the Horn.* The rider dives off over the saddle-horn and does not touch the ground, but holds his tuck and muscles himself *back over the horn* to finish astride the saddle.

67—*Horn Cartwheels or Pinwheel Cartwheels.* The rider goes forward over the horn as in No. 66, but touches the ground and continues *around* to raise his feet over the horn to drop forward into another cartwheel.

68—*Spread-eagle Cartwheels.* These are done like No. 67 but from front and rear saddle handholds.

69—*Crossover Cartwheels.* The rider goes from a cartwheel done on one side of the horse to a cartwheel on the opposite side without stopping between them or changing handholds.

70—*Crupper Cartwheel.* The rider jumps from behind his horse to rise in a forward turnover to the side of his mount where his feet hit to lift him back astride his horse's rump.

71—*Straight Crupper or Crupper Jump-ups.* The rider, keeping his legs spread, drops off behind the horse, hits the ground and jumps back astride the horse.

72—*High Cruppers.* The rider starts as in No. 71, but when returning to the horse's back the rider's body goes high, almost to a handstand position.

73—*Crupper Walk.* The rider starts as in No. 71, but does not immediately return to his horse's back but takes long, slow, leisurely steps in a make-believe walk, behind his speeding mount.

74—*Crupper Jump to the Saddle.* Same start as No. 71, but rider jumps to land sitting in the saddle.

75—*Straight Crupper to Reverse in the Saddle.* The rider starts as in No. 74, but turns in the air to land sitting backward in his saddle.

76—*Crupper Drag.* Starts same as No. 71 but rider spreads his legs and drags his feet in the dust.

77—*Crupper Jump to a Stand.* The rider does a straight crupper or high crupper and comes down to his feet or to *one foot* in an upright stand on the horse's rump.

78—*Crupper Jump to a Shoulder Stand.* The rider does a high crupper and alights balanced on his shoulder in the saddle.

79—*Crupper Jump to a Headstand.* Same as No. 78 but rider alights on his head in the saddle.

80—*Crupper Jump to a Backward Tailstand.* Rider does a crupper jump bringing his legs forward under his arms to allow him to roll backward into the tailstand described in No. 46.

81—*High Crupper to a Spread-eagle Cartwheel.* Rider at peak height of crupper jump changes one handhold and falls over into the Spread-eagle Cartwheels, No. 68.

82—*Crupper Leg Over.* The rider crosses one leg over at his peak height and comes down alongside his horse to vault back to the saddle.

83—*Crupper Roll Up to the Saddle.* The rider does the crupper jump, then rolls forward out of it to land facing forward astride the saddle.

84—*Crupper Somersault to the Saddle.* Same as No. 83, only the rider does not *roll* but somersaults forward, *clear* of the horse, to land in the saddle.

85—*Reverse Crupper or Crupper Splits to the Saddle.* The rider facing forward drops to the ground *alongside* the rear of the horse, jumps and twists in the air to land backward in the saddle.

86—*Crupper Splits to the Neck.* Same as No. 85 but rider lands backwards on the neck in front of the saddle.

87—*Crupper Split to a Hip Roll.* The rider lands on his hip back of the saddle and rolls ahead to straddle the saddle facing forward.

88—*Reverse Crupper Float.* Rider rises from the ground, facing up as he goes over the back of the horse to land in a forward position in the saddle.

89—*Crupper Split to a Straight.* Same as No. 85, but the rider crosses his legs (scissors them) to enable him to land *straight* or facing forward in the saddle.

90—*Reverse Crupper to Sideways in the Saddle.* Same as No. 88, but the rider keeps both legs together and lands in a sideways position in the saddle.

91—*The Ferris Wheel.* The rider starts as in No. 90 but goes *clear over* the saddle to return to the *starting* point for a repeat.

92—*Reverse Crupper Roll Ups.* The rider starts from the *reverse crupper* but does a roll up finishing forward in the saddle as in No. 83.

93—*Reverse Crupper to a Tailstand.* The rider starts a reverse crupper but jumps from the ground directly into a tailstand No. 45.

94—*The Billy Keen Drag.* The rider drags his feet behind the horse as he hangs on facing backward over the tail of his horse.

95—*The Ted Elder Drag.* Differs from No. 94 in that the rider's head is out of sight between the horse's hind legs.

96—*The Elder Tail Drag Layout.* Same start as No. 95, but the rider *holds the horizontal position* he gets just before his feet touch the ground for the drag.

97—*The Side Drag.* Same as No. 94, but the rider drags off to one side and not directly over the tail.

98—*Spread-eagle Drag.* Spread-eagled alongside his horse, the rider drags one foot, the other being in the stirrup as he hangs from one rear handhold.

99—*Going Under the Neck.* The rider passes beneath the neck of his horse going down from one side of the saddle on one side and coming up from the other.

100—*Going Under the Belly.* The rider passes beneath the horse from one side to return to the saddle from the other.

101—*Going Between the Hind Legs from Below.* The rider passes through the horse's hind legs from below and does a crupper mount to return to his horse's back.

102—*Going Between the Hind Legs from Above.* The rider uses a different rigging and system from No. 101, and does not touch the ground, as he travels from the top of his horse's back and down, to pass through the hind legs and return to the saddle.

103—*The Slick Saddle Stand.* Upright stands are in three catagories: 1: Strap Stands, those done with the feet secured; 2: Slick Stands, those done from free-to-move feet as the rider holds his balance with the reins or a strap from the saddle; 3: Free stands, these are, as the word implies, entirely free, no aids, only balance, enable the rider to accomplish them. The Slick Saddle Stand rider stands straight in the saddle holding the reins or thong from the saddle.

104—*Slick Stand Over the Hips.* The rider stands as in No. 103, but on the rump of the horse.

105—*One-foot Slick Saddle Stand.* The rider stands as in No. 103, but on only *one* foot.

106—*One-foot Slick Stand Over the Hips.* Same as No. 104, but the rider balances on one foot.

107—*Backward One-foot Slick Saddle Stand.* Rider stands backwards in the saddle on one foot.

108—*Free Stand in the Saddle.* Same as No. 103, but rider has both hands free. It is also done while the rider stands on the rear jockeys.

109—*Free Stand on the Rump.* Same as No. 104, but rider does not hold on.

110—*Sideways Free Stand With One Foot on the Horse's Neck.* Rider stands with one foot in the saddle the other being held high up on the horse's neck.

111—*Cantle and Horn Free Stand.* The rider stands sideways with one foot on the saddle cantle, the other on the horn.

112—*Backward Free Stand.* Rider is backward, but free as he rides on on the rump or in the saddle.

113—*Free Stand Pirouette.* The rider does a free stand, then jumps and twists to alight facing the opposite direction.

114—*Headstand in the Saddle.* Rider is facing backward standing on his head in the saddle.

115—*Backward Headstand in the Saddle.* Self-explanatory, being opposite of No. 114.

116—*Headstand on the Saddle Horn.*

117—*Headstand on the Side Jockey.* This is a sideways headstand done on the side of the saddle.

118—*Headstand on the Rump.* The rider stands on his head on the rump facing forward.

119—*Roll to the Neck from a Crupper Scissors.* The rider starts with No. 41, then rolls over the horn to a backward position on the neck of his horse.

120—*Back Roll to a Crupper Jump.* The rider, sitting normally in the saddle, rolls straight over backward to land behind his horse in position for his crupper jump return to horseback.

121—*Standing Back Somersault to a Crupper Jump.* The rider stands, turns a back somersault to the ground and does a crupper jump back to the horse.

122—*The "Possum Belly" Ride.* The rider lies horizontally and face downward beneath the horse and has both hands free.

123—*The "Cradle" Ride.* The rider is beneath the horse as in No. 122 but face up.

124—*Stirrup Spin.* The rider stands in one stirrup, then moves the other leg back, out and completely around, to pass over the horn, returning the rider to the saddle. This is also done by the rider turning around in the opposite direction.

125—*The Walk Over.* Rider stands in one stirrup, raises other leg forward over the saddle, then brings it back between him and the fender to straddle the saddle again. It is also done in the opposite direction.

126—*The Stick Ride.* Rider crosses stirrup over saddle, inserts stick, then straddles this facing outward in a sideways position to ride with both hands and feet outstretched.

127—*Stick Ride Back Bend.* Same start as No. 126, but rider straddles stirrup while facing the horse, then does backbend out from the side of the horse.

128—*Knee Drag from a Stick.* Rider starts as in No. 127, but the stick is beneath the knees as the rider goes over backwards to a drag.

129—*Knee Drag from Horn.* Rider hangs or drags with hands free, with one knee clamped around the saddle horn,

130—*Nancy Bragg Back Bend.* The rider does a back bend, somewhat like a wrestler's "bridge", over the saddle.

131—*Black's Spread-eagle Drag off the Neck.* Rider drags outward from one leg hooked high up over horse's neck, and one saddle handhold.

132—*The Pick Up.* Rider leans down and picks up objects from the ground.

133—*The Step Off or Foot Drag.* The rider steps off to the ground with one foot, drags it in the dust, or alternately gets a vaulting lift with it to return to the saddle.

134—*Barbara Huntington Ballerina Stand.* The rider stands in one stirrup does a split with the leg held against the rider's head with one hand and rides with other hand free.

135—*Side Sitting Arm Drag.* The rider holds on over the saddle, with one hand, and maintains a sideways position facing outward with the feet held horizontally.

136—*Handstand to a Billy Keen Drag.* Rider falls out of a forward facing handstand into the No. 94 drag.

137—*The Jimmy Richardson Layout.* The rider has handholds at both front and rear of the saddle and goes into a horizontal position, face up under the belly of the horse.

138—*Tailstand to a Keen Drag.* Rider does a No. 45 tailstand and raises upward to fall directly into the drag.

139—*The Crossover Roll.* The rider, from a backward position on the horse's neck, drops off to the right side of the horse, hits, lifts and rolls over back of the saddle to hit on the left side, to lift back astride the neck in the starting position.

140—*The Cheyenne Crossover.* The rider drops to the ground alongside the saddle, gets his lift and dives, going sideways completely over the saddle to land in a face-up drag, and lifts from this to land backward on the horse's neck.

141—*Reverse Crupper to a Backward Stand in the Saddle.* The rider does a reverse crupper No. 85 but instead of landing astride, he lands on both feet or on one foot as in No. 14.

142—*Tail Ride.* The rider sits straddling a stick inserted through the hair above a knot tied in the horse's tail and rides with his hands outstretched.

143—*The Head Ride.*

144—*Spin from the Rump to the Neck.*

# B. HALF A CENTURY OF PROFESSIONAL TRICK RIDERS

## MEN

Buck Abbott
John Agee
Charlie Aldridge
Johnny Baldwin
Ben Beckley
Billy Binder
Jimmy Black
Scotty Black
Art Boden
Paul Bond
Dick Borello
Marco Borello
Buck Bowhan
Ed Bowman
Buff Brady, Sr.
Buff Brady
Bud Brown
Frank Butler
Louis Cabral
Bob Calem
Jack Cavanaugh
Joe Chirwka
Smokey Chism
Ralph Clark
Bobby Clark
Cody Compton
Joe Cook
Dick Corey
Cecil Cornish
Ralph Corpe
Tommy Cropper
Frank Dance
Hank Darnell
Indian Joe Davis
Frank Dean
Danny Dent
Deer Family
Kenneth Foy
Neal Freel
Tim Freel
Freddy Deschamps
Dan Dix
Billie Dorrah
Wild Bill Dunnivan
Buck Eddy
Buckaroo Eddy
Ted ("Suicide") Elder
Charlie Ellet
Billy Epperson
Jim Eskew, Jr.
Lee Ferris ("Canada Kid")
Sam Garrett
Pete Genett
Hoot Gibson

Pinky Gist
Augie Gomez
Vern Goodrich
Bee Hoo Gray
Joe Greer
Harry Greer
Dick Griffith
Ed Guelick
Buster Guelick
Frank Guskey
Gene Hall
Billy Hammond
Ed Harney
Walt Heacock
Bill Held
Byron Hendricks
Lee Hendricks
Pat Henry
Harry Hill
Ray Hill
Herb Hobsins
Gyp Holliday
George Hooker
Chet Howell
Jack Hoxie
Freddie Hunt
Floyd Irwin
LeRoy Johnson
Le Roy (Buff) Jones
Jack Joyce
Billy Keen
Tin Horn Hank Keenan
Tin Horn Hank Keenan, Jr.
Tommy Kiernan
Don Killem
Clyde Kinney
Jim Kinnley
Brent Kirby
Butch Kirby
Sandy Kirby
Johnny Kissinger
Otto Klein
Charlie La Mont
Larry Lansburg
Ike Lewin
Larry Lewis
Joe Loesen
Buck Lucus
Scout Maish
Tod Mason
Ken Maynard
Kermit Maynard
Lloyd McBee
Johnny McCracken

Hank McFarland
Don McLennon
Wilber Zack Miller
Montie Montana
Montie Montana, Jr.
Billy Mossman
Dave Nemo
Nick Nickols
Charlie Nielson
Buck Owens
Dick Pickard
George Pitman
Glenn Porter
Hank Potts
Booger Red Privett
Tommy Privett
Jack Quait
Marvin Ramsey
Ray Ramsey
Montana Jack Ray
Buddy Reager
Harvey Rex
Brown Jug Reynolds
Jimmie Richardson
Bob Rint
Dennis Rivers
Johnny Rivers
Will Rogers
Lonnie Rooney
J. King Ross
Mark Rossi
Rex Rossi
Billy Rowe
Bobby Ruiz
Lee Le Roy
Paul St. Croix
Doc Sahr
Frank Scott
Claude Smith
Corey Smith
Curly Smith
Richard Smith
Drew Stanfield
Dick Stanley
Jason Stanley
Francis Steller
"Ty" Stokes
Earl Strause
Al Stringham
Leonard Stroud
Buck Stuart
Cameron Sullivan
Earl Sutton
Ike Tacker

Charlie Tantlinger
Johnny Tantlinger
Louis Tindall
Harry Walters
Floyd Weaver
Francis Weaver
Fred Wiedermann
Snapper Weiderman
Don Wilcox
Ernie Willits
Jack Williams
Ken Williams

Homer Wilson
Jack Wright
Jitney Wright
Buck Yarbrough
Adams Family
Buzz Carson Family
Graham's Western Riders
Thompson's White Horse
   Ranch Riders
Capt. Fox's New York
   State Troopers

Victor McLaughlin's Black
   Horse Troop

## COSSACKS
Tephon
Ishlah
Prince Willikow
Emily Willikow
Prince Luke
Captain Georgi

## WOMEN

Jenne Abbott
Mickey Adams
Jean Allen
Prairie Lilly Allen
Birdie Askins
Mable Baker
Tillie Baldwin
Ray Beach
Montana Belle
Teeny Binder
Sandra Black
Faye Blackstone
Burtha Blanchard
Faye Blessing
June Borchard
May Boss
Jane Bowhan
Nancy Bragg
June Burchard
Pee Wee Burge
Polly Burson
Bernadette Cabral
Kitty Canutt
Etta Myers Carreon
Jackie Carstens
Sunbeam Chism
Loretta Cosca
Donna Cowan
Gene Creed
Monty Daniels
Bernice Dean
Sparky Dent
Vernee Dobbs
Bernice Dossey
Mildred Douglas
Betty Elliot
Claudia Elliot
Leah Ferris
Evelyn Finley
Nancy Fisher
Helen Gibson
Marie Gibson
Pearl Gist

Myrtle Goodrich
Bonnie Gray
Juanita Gray
Reva Grey
Connie Griffith
Joyce Gusky
Virginia Regar Hadley
Rene Hafley
Donna Hall
Edith Happy
Darlene Harding
Malee Harding
Fox Hastings
Boots Heacock
Eleanor Heacock
Doris Held
Juanita Howell
Thelma Hunt
Barbara Huntington
Mary Iler
Pauline Irwin
Iva Dell Jacobs
Betty Johnson
Dell Befhart Jones
Mary Keen
Bee Kiernan
Dorothy King
Mildred Kirby
Fay Knight
Ted Lamb
Betty Lamb
Kay Lewis
Igge Linsey
Ella Linton
Rose Lorimer
Mitzi Lucus
Sharon Lucus
Shirley Lucus
Tad Lucus
Rose Malally
Ruth Marian
Blanche McBee
Hazel McCart

Vera McGinnis
Midge McLain
Hope McLennon
Anna Lee Mills
Rose La Mont
Louise Montana
Cherrie Moomaw
Percina Clark Morris
Peggy Murry
Dolly Mullins
Alice Nesbitt
Marion Nesbitt
Pauline Nesbitt
Fanny Nielson
Pat North
Helen Panzella
Pat Paul
Ethel Perry
Juanita Perry
Pauline Pickard
Edith Prairie
Ethel Prairie
Alice Privett
Florance Randolph
Dixie Regar
Mildred Rex
Dorothy Looney Ring
Margie Roberts
Betsy King Ross
Christy Lee Roy
Marie St. Croix
Dorothy Saterfield
Betty Saylors
Karen Schappacher
Sharon Schappacher
Della Schriver
Nancy Shepperd
Norma Shoulders
Erma Jean Simon
Francis Simon
Punkin Simson
Alice Sisty
Rose Smith

Wilma Standard
Marjorie Stanfield
Janie Statz
Bobby Steel
Dolores Steelman
Patsy Stout
Verna Stracken
Veldeen Strauss
Sandra Sue Strauss
Mable Strickland
Francis Stroud
Mamie Stroud
Ethel Sullivan
Vicky Sullivan
Mary Sutton

Georgia Sweet
Ruby Tacker
Patty Hall Templeton
Claire Belcher Thompson
Marjorie Thorne
Velma Tindell
Fedalia Tope
Rosemary Tope
Bug Torrence
Pat Torrence
Tinker Tower
Babe Benal Towne
Lorena Trickey
Alice Van
Florence Van

Tillie Van
Dot Vernon
Adele Vinole
Charlene Walling
Rose Washington
Lola White
Marie White
Vivian White
Babe Willets
Lavina Williams
Nicke Williams
Paris Williams
Betty Willis
Norma Young
Zana Zumwalt

*BOYS*
Alan Cartwright
Brad "Butch" Frank
Tad Griffith
Bill McEnaneys
Rusty Riggs
Corey Smith
Jerry Thornton
The "Thunderbirds"

*GIRLS*
Vicky Adams
Cristy Brown
Sheila Frank
Bonny Happy
Cindy Hofmann
Sherry Jean McCarthy
Wendy Orstadius
Melody Packard
Lenore Rowe
Skeeter Ruiz
Doris Schappacher
Edie Smart
Lynda Thornton